THE L

BY

HIS HOLINESS POPE SHENOUDA III

St Shenouda Monastery
Sydney, Australia

The Life of Faith

By His Holiness Pope Shenouda III

Second Edition, January 2019

First Edition August 1989

Revised by COEPA 1997

Fully revised and edited by:
St. Shenouda Monastery
8419 Putty Rd, Putty, NSW, 2330
Australia

ISBN: 978-0-6481234-3-9

Special thanks to all the youth who helped, God reward you all.

Cover Design by Jonathan Grace

CONTENTS

In the name of the Father and of the Son and of the Holy Spirit, One God. Amen.

INTRODUCTION

Faith is not merely adopting a set of beliefs that you may say in the 'Creed', but a way of life or adherence to that which leads to life.

To what benefit is believing in God without having a relationship with Him, obeying and loving Him?

In addition, what is the benefit of believing in eternity and in life after death if one does not prepare for it by repentance, spiritual vigil, and loving God?

And to what benefit is believing in virtues if one does not live them? Therefore there is a big difference between theoretical faith, which does not save the soul and practical faith, the fruits of which are evident in one's life.

This book was written to explain to you the meaning of faith, its stages and types and its importance in our lives and its greatness.

St. Paul wrote, *"Examine yourselves as to whether you are in the faith. Test yourselves. Do you not know yourselves...."* (2 Cor.13:5). Not everyone who says he believes has faith but faith is measured according to God's saying, *"...You will know them by their fruits."* (Matt. 7:16).

There are those who claim to have faith but have neither the heart nor the life of a believer. So what then is the life of a believer?
The life of faith is linked with peace, tranquility and lack of fear, for when you become afraid, the Lord will say to you, *"O you of*

little faith, why did you doubt?" (Matt. 14:31).

The life of a believer is also associated with purity of behaviour, for the believer feels the presence of God, who sees, hears and records all that he does. For this reason the believer feels ashamed and afraid of doing wrong in front of God.

The life of a believer is a life of submission to the will of God. Having faith that God is the maker of all things and all that He permits to happen is for our own good. In this way, God's children live in peace, happiness and satisfaction with all that God grants them.

The life of faith believes anything is possible for the Lord, who said, *"All things are possible to him who believes."* (Mark 9:23). Therefore the believer does not quiver in times of distress, but believes wholeheartedly that God has many solutions and will interfere to fulfill His will.

The believer does not enter into an argument with God about what He is doing but accepts all things with confidence in God's wisdom and love. The believer concentrates on the unseen more than what is visible to his eyes, *"...For the things which are seen are temporary, but the things which are not seen are eternal."* (2 Cor.4:18).

The heroes of faith are not only those who defended their faith but also those who lived a fruitful life of faith that worked in love.

This book before you, will clarify the life of faith, how it is acquired and how to test if you are really in faith or not.

Pope Shenouda III

CHAPTER 1

HOW GREAT IS FAITH

The importance of faith is clearly seen in the Apostle's words, *"...But without faith it is impossible to please Him."* (Heb.11:6).

The importance of faith also shows in the Apostle's classification of faith as one of the three great virtues, *"...faith, hope and love..."* (1 Cor.13:13). The Apostle also describes the importance of faith in the life of righteousness, *"Now the just shall live by faith..."* (Heb.10:38).

Faith is the beginning of the road which leads to God.

For how can you be united with God and God with you, to walk with Him and keep His commandments, if first you do not believe in His existence, His divinity or in His book (the Bible) and all that it contains?

Thus faith is the beginning of the road to God and essential for salvation, as the Lord Himself said, *"He who believes and is baptised will be saved."* (Mark 16:16). *"...That whoever believes in Him should not perish but have everlasting life."* (John 3:16). *"He who believes in Him is not condemned; but he who does not believe is condemned already."* (John 3:18). He also reprimanded the Jews by saying, *"...you will die in your sins; ... if you do not believe that I am He..."* (John 8:24).

Salvation is available to everyone through the blood of our Lord Jesus but it cannot save without faith, as St. Paul and Silas said to the jail keeper, *"Believe on the Lord Jesus Christ, and you will be saved, you and your household."* (Acts 16:31).

Through this faith, the Gospels were written and preached by the Apostles.

John the evangelist, inspired by the Holy Spirit, wrote, *"...but these are written that you may believe that Jesus is the Christ, the Son of God, and that believing you may have life in His name"* (John 20:31).

Faith is the beginning of a life with God. Faith is also our companion throughout our lives. Faith is very important for a life of righteousness. The Apostles wrote about the righteousness which is credited to faith, *"By his faith he condemned the world and became heir of the righteousness that comes by faith."* (Heb. 11:7). Also, *"...And it was credited to him as righteousness"* (James 2:23). The Bible also speaks of justification by faith, *"Therefore, having been justified by faith, we have peace with God through our Lord Jesus Christ."* (Rom.5:1).

Faith is a necessary for miracles and their acceptance.

How great is our Lord's saying to the blind man of Jericho, *"Your faith has healed you..."* (Luke 18:42, Mark 10:52). Also His saying to the man with leprosy, *"...Your faith has made you well."* (Luke 17:19). To the sick woman He said, *"Be of good cheer, daughter; your faith has made you well"* (Matt. 9:22). When He heard the two blind men shouting, *"Have mercy on us, Son of David. "*(Matt. 9:27), He said to them, *"According to your faith let it be to you"* (Matt. 9:29) and their sight was restored.
On the other hand, we see that the Lord in His hometown, *"...did not do many miracles there because of their lack of faith."* (Matt. 13:58).

The power of God can do miracles for you but it awaits your faith.

He will grant you according to your faith. For this reason miracles happen to some and not to others, although the power of God is the same.

What about he, who is weak in faith? He has to pray as did the boy's father who said, *"Lord, I believe; help my unbelief!"* (Mark 9:24). Here we see that God performs miracles in general according to faith but on other occasions, He performs miracle that we may believe. In both cases faith is coupled with the miracle, either it comes before or is caused by it.

Faith, regardless of type, is a source of power.

It is sufficient that when a person believes in an idea, you see them working with Christ's power to carry it through. Faith gives them perseverance, might and courage which they would not have otherwise.

Thus, where there is faith, there is power. A prayer with faith is a strong prayer. He who believes in prayer and its effects, prays with fervor, assurance and power. A sermon preached by a person who believes in every word, makes a strong sermon, and through it, his faith is transmitted to the hearts of his listeners.

The importance of faith lies in its association with many virtues.

The fruits of faith are; strength, peace, courage, tranquility and comfort. Through faith we gain; a life of purity and righteousness, a life of submission and devotion to God, a life of prayer and many other virtues.

A few questions then come to mind:

- What is faith?
- Why is faith, the basis of salvation and redemption?
- What type of faith is it that leads to all the virtues?
- What type of faith is it that can perform miracles and wonders of

which our Lord describes saying, *"Everything is possible for him who believes"* (Mark 9:23)?

CHAPTER 2

WHAT IS FAITH?

Any worshipper of God can use the word 'faith' even when he does not believe in the Truth.

He may have the name of a believer but does not have the heart of one.

Faith does not automatically make you a believer, even if you are born in a family which believes in the existence of God. Faith has a much deeper meaning than this, it encompasses the whole spiritual life and performs miracles.

On one occasion, the disciples of the Lord were unable to heal an epileptic boy from a demon, so they asked the Lord for the reason and He answered them, *"Because of your unbelief."* (Matt. 17:20). The Lord rebuked them by saying, *"O faithless and perverse generation"* (Matt 17:17).

God came for a generation of unbelievers but were they really unbelievers? How alarming! Here the Lord says to His disciples, *"I say to you, if you have faith as a mustard seed, you will say to this mountain, `Move from here to there,' and it will move"* (Matt. 17:20).

Truly, what is this faith of a seed which can move a mountain?

As the Apostle's say, *"Examine yourselves as to whether you are in the faith. Test yourselves"* (2 Cor. 13:5).

The Bible informs us of a dangerous state that we need to be aware of. It is the state of a human being who seems to be believing in God, he prays and performs miracles but he does not believe in the Truth and isn't even accepted in the eyes of God! Here is what the

Lord Himself said, *"Not everyone who says to Me, `Lord, Lord,' shall enter the kingdom of heaven..."* (Matt 7:21). The Lord continues, *"Many will say to Me in that day, `Lord, have we not prophesied in Your name, cast out demons in Your name, and done many wonders in Your name?' And then I will declare to them, `I never knew you; depart from Me, you who practice lawlessness!'"* (Matt.7:22-23).

What shall we call those who say, 'Lord, Lord... in your name we did this and that'? Are they really believers?
Maybe it's only an apparent faith, or faith by name, or only mental faith but it's not the true faith that is accepted by God.

What then is this real faith that is accepted in the eyes of the Lord? We ask Him and He answers, *"Not everyone who says to Me, `Lord, Lord,' ... but he who does the will of My Father in heaven"* (Matt. 7:21). This also reminds us of the story of the five virgins who also used the expression, 'Lord, Lord,...' when they stood behind the closed door saying, *"Lord, Lord open the door for us"* (Matt. 25:11), and they heard from the Lord the clear and terrifying answer, *"I tell you the truth, I don't know you."* (Matt. 25:12).

The expression 'Lord, Lord', does not necessarily help if you are awaiting the bridegroom with a lamp without oil, or if you arrive after the door is closed.

Therefore what is faith? What is its connection to oil which signifies the Holy Spirit? What is its connection with the will of God who is in heaven?

This faith is alive and is accepted by God as we'll see later... Faith is not simply a belief but also a way of life.

You can test it by its fruits in your life... as the Lord said, *"You will know them by their fruits....every good tree bears good fruit, but a bad tree bears bad fruit. Therefore by their fruits you will know them."* (Matt. 7:16-20).

This is how you can test your faith; does your faith bear fruit? As our Lord said, *"Therefore by their fruits you will know them".* *(Matt. 7:20)*

This is what John the Evangelist teaches us, *"Now by this we know that we know Him"*... how? *"If we keep His commandments. He who says, "I know Him," and does not keep His commandments, is a liar, and the truth is not in him"* (1 John 2:3-4). Faith is tested through a life of obedience to God's commandments and he who does not have this obedience is not considered a believer of Truth and cannot claim to know God.

The Apostle Paul lists in his letter to the Hebrews (Heb. 11) wonderful examples of faithful men. They showed practical faith in their private lives. Enoch for example; the Bible did not say that he defended his belief like other heroes of faith. Enoch was a hero of faith because, *"...he pleased God."* (Heb. 11:5) and *"...walked with God."* (Gen. 5:22, 24).

You may not be as spiritually knowledgeable as were the Apostles but no doubt you can also lead the same life as our father Enoch, who walked with God. You can live like other men of faith whom St. Paul mentioned, *"They were strangers and pilgrims on the earth... they desire a better, that is, a heavenly country."* (Heb 11:13,16).

Our father Abraham was a man of faith who, *"Obeyed when he was called to go out"* (Heb. 11:8), and went out after God, *"Not knowing where he was going."* (Heb. 11:8) He was a man of faith in accepting God's timing and being obedient to God. Even when he was asked to sacrifice his only son, he was confident that God can raise him from the dead (Heb. 11:17-19).

His wife Sarah is also considered a hero of faith because she believed the Lord for *"She judged Him faithful who had promised."* (Heb 11:11).

Heroes of faith are not only those who defended their belief but are also those who believed in the Lord, walked with Him, who were righteous and pleased Him (Heb. 11:33). Also those who, *"Were tortured, not accepting deliverance, that they might obtain a better resurrection, ..."* and those who, *"had trial of mockings and scourgings, yes, and of chains and imprisonment... of whom the world was not worthy... "* (Heb.11:35-38), *"And all these, having obtained a good testimony through faith"* (Heb. 11:39). In all these examples, the Bible gives us a wide spectrum of the meaning of faith.

St. Paul tells us that faith, *"Is the substance of things hoped for, the evidence of things not seen"* (Heb. 11:1).

You hope for many things after death. You hope for eternal life with the angels and saints and to see the Lord in Paradise and resurrection from the dead into a spiritual body. You desire eternal peace after the general resurrection. Faith is to believe in these without having any doubt. Faith is complete confidence that these matters exist without having seen them.

Faith Is Beyond the Level of Our Senses

Faith does not contradict but is beyond our senses. Faith is a higher power than our limited senses. Our senses are only capable of detecting physical or materialistic things but there are other matters that are beyond the material sense. The senses are also limited in what they can physically detect.

Instruments are often used to sense details and gain information which the senses alone cannot accomplish. How much more is it for the non-physical, which the Apostle called, "invisible things"? Faith is not what is seen by the human eye (2 Cor. 5:7). The soul cannot be seen or felt by the senses. The fact that the senses do not feel the soul does not mean that it does not exist but rather it is unable to be detected. The senses are limited in scope when observing things to do with the soul.

Faith Is Beyond the Level of the Intellect

Intellect may guide you to the beginning of the way but faith continues with you on the way to the end. Faith does not contradict intellect but leads it to a higher level that the mind alone cannot reach.

What the mind cannot understand is called unattainable. We often describe God as infinite because He has no limit. The human mind is limited and can only understand the limited matters. The mind can bring you to know God and some of His qualities but faith is what, *"God has revealed... to us through His Spirit."* (1 Cor. 2:10). God reveals Himself to the believer only to the extent that they can bear to comprehend.

The mind may not grasp many things but must accept them. By nature, the mind does not refuse all that it does not understand. There are for example, in our physical world, many inventions only experts can understand. In spite of this, the normal mind can accept and deal with these things, without knowing how they work. The mind accepts death and speaks about it but does not understand it.

If the mind accepts many things in our world without understanding them, then clearly nothing should deprive the mind from accepting other matters not of this world.

The mind does not understand how miracles happen but it accepts them and finds joy in them.

A miracle is called a miracle because the mind fails to grasp it and cannot explain it but the mind accepts it by faith. This faith, with infinite power, greater than that of the mind, can perform things the mind fails to understand. This power is the power of God the almighty.

We respect the mind and at the same time we know its limits. We cannot accept the proud mind that desires to understand all things and will not acknowledge that there are some things that are beyond our comprehension.

The mind should be humble and know its limitations; *"For I say, through the grace given to me, to everyone who is among you, not to think of himself more highly than he ought to think, but to think soberly, as God has dealt to each one a measure of faith. "* (Rom. 12.3). The mind should submit matters beyond its level of understanding to faith.

If the mind wanted to nullify all that it does not understand, it would end up destroying itself, losing the element of faith and put itself in a very narrow circle of understanding.

Believers are moderate, they esteem the mind and use it in religious and spiritual affairs. There are philosophers and people of high intellect among the believers who do not depend only on the mind, or trust in its ability to understand all things. However, in simplicity and humility they confess that their minds are limited and are unable to understand all that is associated with God. With faith, their hearts and minds accept all that is beyond the level of the mind.

The simple and humble mind accepts faith and miracles.

We mean humble in the sense that the mind is not proud of its own understanding or rejects all that is does not understand. It does not complicate matters or insist on placing everything within its own limits. We will refer to this point later when we speak about the simplicity of faith.

Faith is not only a prayer said but a life we live. If you are living a life of faith, the fruits of faith are apparent in your practical life. Examine your faith by the virtues you live by in your life. As the Apostle says, *"Examine yourselves as to whether you are in the faith"* (2 Cor. 13:5).

Conviction of the Unseen

The Apostles said this about faith; *"Faith is the substance of things hoped for, the evidence of things not seen."* (Heb. 11:1). We want to know what this verse means!

Conviction is certainty, confidence and belief without doubt. It is not simply an idea, opinion or knowledge gained from reading or hearing about it but certainty that unseen matters exist.

Here is a clear difference between believers and men of science. The things that are not seen are not in the working field of the researchers. If they are not sure of something, they investigate it thoroughly with their instruments and apparatus. The same also applies to men of material beliefs.

Believers are not like this, they follow God's saying, *"Blessed are those who have not seen and yet have believed"* (John 20:29).

The believer accepts the creation from nothing. The scientists refuse this matter. They cannot believe that five loaves of bread fed five thousand men (excluding the women and children) and that twelve baskets full of bread were left over. The believer accepts all this.

The believer accepts firstly that God is powerful. He also accepts everything in a certain range of this unlimited power.

The believer frees himself from the doubts of researchers and the investigations of the unbelievers. Not only does he accept the unseen but he lives according to and focuses his mind and affection on the unseen according to the Apostle's words, *"While we do not look at the things which are seen, but at the things which are not seen. For the things which are seen are temporary, but the things which are not seen are eternal."* (2 Cor. 4:18).

You will ask, 'How can I see the hidden'? The answer is, by faith. What are then those unseen matters? The first is God Himself, His qualities, His works and all things pertaining to Him.

1. God, His Qualities and Works

God is unseen, as John the evangelist said, *"No one has seen God..."* (John 1:18). Actually who can see the Divinity? No one! However, in spite of this, you believe in Him with all your heart and with all certainty. This faith does not at all rely on your physical senses. You may say you see Him with your trained spiritual senses (Heb.5:14). Non-physical senses were trained to see the unseen and we have the following examples from the Bible:

David said, *"I have set the Lord always before me; because He is at my right hand I shall not be moved."* (Ps 16:8). So how did he see the Lord in front of him and at his right hand at all times? No doubt he saw Him with an eye of faith. In some of the translations it is written, *"I have seen the Lord...."*, that means that he is continuously seeing the unseen and focusing on Him with mind and feeling.

With the same meaning Elijah said, *"As the Lord of hosts lives, before whom I stand."* (1 Kin 18:15). How was he able to feel that he stands before God? How was he able to always see the Lord in front of him? It is by faith that the Lord is before him, and not through the bodily senses since they cannot arouse a believer's heart. It is faith that sees the unseen.

If you are in faith, you will have confidence that God is always before you and will act according to this belief, that God sees you and hears you...

If you live in faith, you are sure that God is in the midst of His people, according to His promise, *"...I am there in the midst of them"* (Matt. 18:20) and *"I am with you always, even to the end of the age."* (Matt.28:20). You do not see Him with the eye of your body but you believe that He is in our midst. You do not need to see Him physically to believe. You believe without seeing, or you perceive the unseen.

What is a spiritual life my brothers and sisters? Is it not simply a shift in belief from what is felt and visible to the unseen.

We live with the assurance of the unseen things, with confidence that God is in front of us. This becomes the difference between the believer and the non- believer.

The non-believer desires to see everything with his eyes, or else he cannot believe. The believer does not allow his eyes, senses, or external happenings shape his beliefs. His heart believes in the existence of unseen matters. On one occasion God rebuked His disciple Thomas who would not believe without seeing when He said to him, *"Do not be unbelieving, but believing."* and *"...Because you have seen Me, you have believed. Blessed are those who have not seen and yet have believed."* (John 20:27, 29).

We mentioned earlier that faith in God is belief in unseen matters. Not only faith in the existence of God but also faith in His attributes and in His works.

You believe in His goodness and that His choices for you are for the best. You trust that He is the Almighty who has dominion over all things. You believe that He is able to do everything for, *"The things which are impossible with men are possible with God."* (Luke 18:27). You believe in God's love for you and for others.

You may not see all these qualities physically but you believe in them. You believe that God takes care of the universe and preserves its beauty. You believe that He labours and takes care of every individual. You will either see His work or the results of His work or you will not see anything at all.

2. The Timing of God

The following describes men of faith; *"These all died in faith, not having received the promises, but having seen them afar off were assured of them, embraced them and confessed that they were strangers and pilgrims on the earth."* (Heb.11:13). These people waited for the things promised in faith and believed in what the Lord said to them.

The promises of God, *"....which God has prepared for those who love Him."* (1 Cor. 2:9), were all unseen matters, as explained by the Apostle, *"Eye has not seen, nor ear heard, nor have entered into the heart of man...."* (1 Cor. 2:9).

God's warnings are also unseen things. Noah believed the Lord when He said that He will send a flood over the whole world even though floods were unknown to Noah. No flood had ever happened in his days or the days of his ancestors. However he believed that this flood would happen. He laboured to complete the ark, enduring mockery from others; these were years of faith.

Noah heeded the warning of God and was therefore considered a man of faith. Through faith he had seen the flood before it happened. Through faith, he entered the ark with his wife, his sons and his son's wives. Our teacher Saint Paul teaches us, *"By faith*

Noah, being divinely warned of things not yet seen, moved with godly fear, prepared an ark for the saving of his household." (Heb. 11:7). The others who did not heed God's warning and had no faith in God's truth, were destroyed.

Lot and the city of Sodom also experienced God's warning. When God said that He would destroy these cities only Lot believed Him. Lot believed even though he had never heard of fire coming down from heaven. The people of Sodom, who did not accept the warning of God suffered the same fate as the people at the time of Noah and were destroyed.

God's warning in regard to eternity and judgment is ever before us. In spite of this, many are still immersed in evil and sin as if God had not warned them. They do not fear God in their hearts or judgment for eternity.

We spoke about God, His attributes and works, His promises and His warnings as unseen matters. We should also add:

3. The Dwelling of the Holy Spirit and His Work in us Are Unseen Matters.

Samuel anointed David with oil and the Spirit of the Lord came upon him (2 Sam. 16:13). No one saw the Spirit of the Lord but it happened.

No one was able to see the Holy Spirit descend on the new believers when the Disciples placed their hands on them (Acts 8:17). The Holy Spirit also came on others (1 John 2:20, 27). No one saw the Holy Spirit but its fruits showed in their life.

You may be aware that there is an inner power working in you and for you, yet you do not see it. The Lord foretold this, *"...But you shall receive power when the Holy Spirit has come upon you...."*

(Acts 1:8). This power, the power of the Holy Spirit, guides you to do good, helps you and protects you from sin. Our whole life becomes a fellowship with the Holy Spirit (2 Cor. 13:14).

What is this fellowship with the Holy Spirit? How does it take place? How can we be in fellowship with the Godly nature, an unseen nature? We believe in God's active spirit working in the church, we do not see it but we believe in it.

The Apostle said, *"Do you not know that you are the temple of God and that the Spirit of God dwells in you?"* (1 Cor.3:16), also, *"Do you not know that your body is the temple of the Holy Spirit who is in you, whom you have from God?"* (1 Cor. 6:19).

We do not see the Spirit but we see its fruits.

The Lord said that through the fruits of the Holy Spirit, we can stand before governors and kings, *"For it is not you who speak, but the Spirit of your Father who speaks in you"* (Matt. 10:20). How does the Spirit of the Father speak through us? All these things are unseen matters.

4. The Grace Of God In Us Is Unseen.

We attain visits of grace, which fill us with God's love. We do not see it but we feel it. Grace working in us is without doubt, the work of unseen things.

Saint John the Evangelist said, *"...grace and truth came through Jesus..."* (John 1: 17). What is this grace working in us? And the grace that Saint John enjoyed. St Paul wrote, *"But by the grace of God I am what I am, and His grace toward me was not in vain;..."* (1 Cor. 15:10) and he also says about us, *"For sin shall not have dominion over you, for you are not under law but under grace."* (Rom. 6:14). He also urges Timothy to, *"Be strong in the grace that is in Christ Jesus....*" (2 Tim. 2: 1).

We do not see this grace with our physical eyes, it is amongst the unseen matters but we feel its presence in our lives. The grace of God in us is beyond our senses, as we accept this grace from God. The church grants grace every time it repeats Saint Paul's words, *"The grace of the Lord Jesus Christ, and the love of God, and the communion of the Holy Spirit be with you all."* (2Cor. 13:14).

Here we move to another point, the element of blessings.

5. Blessing Are Unseen

A blessing can be directly from God, from parents, from the church, through the priest etc. All these are unseen matters.

God said to Abraham father of fathers, *"I will make you a great nation; I will bless you and make your name great; And you shall be a blessing. I will bless those who bless you ... And in you all the families of the earth shall be blessed."* (Gen.12:2,3). Abraham saw the fruits of these unseen blessings in his life. Isaac blessed his son Jacob and he became blessed. Esau lamented because he lost this blessing (Gen.27). Jacob blessed Ephraim and Manasseh by saying, *"The Angel who has redeemed me from all evil, Bless the lads."* (Gen. 48:16). Ephraim became exceedingly blessed, more than his brother when Jacob placed his right hand on Ephraim's head (Gen. 48:17-20).

What is this blessing? How was it passed from the hands of Isaac and Jacob? How was it given through the Apostles and from the hands of the men of faith?

We believe in all these unseen matters and in its blessings, although we do not see them. We ask for blessings from our mothers, fathers, from priests and men of God. Abraham was a blessing to the world according to the Lord's promise to him.

Joseph was also a blessing in the house of his master and to all Egypt, as was the blessings of Elijah.

Through all the above examples, we would still be unable to give a precise meaning to the word blessings, for it has a wider meaning than our limited vocabulary can describe. Blessings are an unseen matter of which we can only see its fruits. However, a blessing itself, who can see it and define it?

How was Jesus Christ able to bless through His hands the five loaves of bread and the two fish? This food provided enough to feed thousands of people and despite this, twelve full baskets were left over? How did this happen? What were the causes and its effect? All these things are unseen matters.

6. Faith In The Presence Of Angels and Their Works

We believe in the existence of angels and the unseen spirits. We may not have seen an angel in our whole life but despite this, we believe they are close to us, *"The angel of the Lord encamps all around those who fear Him, And delivers them."*, (Ps 34:7). We believe that the angels fill the church, and have confidence that they are with us in all that we do; *"Are they not all ministering spirits sent forth to minister for those who will inherit salvation?"* (Heb. 1:14).

Many are glad if they see the Virgin Mary or the saints in a revelation. It is far greater to believe that they are around you without seeing them. It is not necessary that God sends you a white dove during your evening church meetings. You should believe without seeing that the church is full of the spirits of angels and that the spirits of the saints hover around us, the saints that God sent to serve humanity.

Gehazi the disciple of Elisha, was afraid when he saw the enemies surrounding the city but Elisha, the man with eyes of faith saw the angels defending it against the enemy. He comforted his disciple by saying, *"Do not fear, for those who are with us are more than those who are with them."* (2 Kin 6:16). Elisha prayed that God would open the eyes of Gehazi to see and grant him conviction in unseen matters.

7. Belief in the Spirit and the Other World

We cannot see the spirit but presume its existence. When a person dies, we say that his spirit, which we have not seen, has left his body.

Faith is concerned with the destiny of this spirit, if it will go to heaven or to hell. Likewise, with the return of this spirit to the body in the general resurrection and the destiny of the resurrected person in eternity after the last judgment.

All these matters, the spirit, resurrection, eternity, judgment, heaven, grace, hell are all unseen matters and through faith we have a conviction in those things. Actually, no one can speak about the eternal life and all things associated with it, except by faith. They believe in life after death though it is an unseen matter.

8. People Believed In the Coming of Christ without Seeing Him

Even the Samaritan woman said to the Lord, *"I know that Messiah is coming..."* (who is called Christ); *"When He comes, He will tell us all things."* (John 4:25).

Thus, everyone knew, according to God's promise that the Messiah was coming. They were eagerly waiting for Him. They understood what Isaiah had said, *"Behold, the virgin shall conceive and bear a Son, and shall call His name Immanuel."* (Isaiah 7:14). They believed although they never saw the Virgin.

The hope and looking for the Messiah of the Old Testament people through faith is like our waiting for the Second Coming of Christ in the New Testament. Our waiting for Christ's Second Coming on the clouds is according to the Lord's promise (Mat. 24:25) and the proclamation of the two angels who appeared to the Disciples (Acts 1:11).

We probably have not seen the Lord on the clouds in the glory of His Father and His saints but through faith, we believe that His Second Coming will be like this.

9. Redemption Is Also From the Unseen Matters

Jesus redeemed us by taking away all our sins and dying for us because of His love, *"All we like sheep have gone astray; We have turned, every one, to his own way; And the Lord has laid on Him the iniquity of us all."* (Isaiah 53:6). John the Baptist also said about Him, *"Behold! The Lamb of God who takes away the sin of the world!"* (John 1:29). John the evangelist said, *"And He Himself is the propitiation for our sins, and not for ours only but also for the whole world."* (1 John 2:2). St. Paul said, *"....having wiped out the handwriting of requirements that was against us..."* (Col.2:14) and *"...having made peace through the blood of His cross...."* (Col. 1:20).

We only see the cross; some may see it as curse! All the gifts the cross has given us of love, redemption, forgiveness, cancelling of the written code, taking away the sins of the world, etc. and also that the cross gave us reconciliation and peace, all these are unseen matters. We see them through faith.

Peter - before believing in all this - saw the cross as loss and as shame! Therefore he said, *"...never, Lord..."* (John 16:22). The Lord rebuked him because Peter did not see the unseen matters.

The cross represents the goodness of God to us. The rulers at that time did not see this because their eyes were blinded, *"...for had they known, they would not have crucified the Lord of glory."* (1 Cor. 2:8).

10. The Hidden Benevolences of God

We only thank God for the benevolences we see and know. However, there are also unseen things we should thank Him for. When we enter the life of faith we automatically enter in a life of perpetual appreciation, as the Apostle said, *"....giving thanks always for all things to God the Father in the name of our Lord Jesus Christ,..."* (Eph. 5:20).

In our life we also have to give thanks for the temptations, because we feel that they have hidden benevolences in them from God that we do not see. If we saw them we'll no doubt be singing with St James the Apostle, *"Count it all joy when you fall into various trials...."* (James 1:2).

From this, we see that faith gives a spiritual meaning to suffering. God allows us to suffer pain for the special grace that is in them. All are unseen matters but we accept them in faith having confidence in God's love, who always does good. We also have confidence in what the Bible says, *"...we know that all things work together for good to those who love God...."* (Rom. 8:28).

11. The Existence Of God In Our Lives And His Power Working In Us.

How beautiful is the Lord's saying to Jacob, *"I am with you and will keep you wherever you go, and will bring you back to this land."* (Gen. 28:15). The Lord was with him and watched over him wherever he went, although he had not seen the Lord physically. It is very comforting for the soul to feel that the Lord is with us and to believe it. This allows us to live in serenity and joy.

The above was not only a blessing to Jacob but the Lord says, *"I am with you always, even to the end of the age."* (Matt. 28:20).

Our feeling that God is with us, gives us a feeling that a Godly power is walking with us and protecting us.

This power is working in you and is with you from the moment you receive the Holy Spirit and He then accompanies you for the rest of your life. In the time of the first church the people saw the kingdom of God being established with power (Mark 9:1), *"...And they were all filled with the Holy Spirit, and they spoke the word of God with boldness."* (Acts 4:31). It was said that St. Stephen was *"....full of faith and power, did great wonders and signs."* (Acts 6:8) and that he stood before the synagogue, *"....And they were not able to resist the wisdom and the Spirit by which he spoke..."* (Acts 6: 10). That is the power of faith. He who believes but is afraid to show his faith is a person with weak faith, he does not believe in the power of God working with him.

The woman who was bleeding for twelve years felt that if she could just touch the edge of the cloak of Jesus, a power would come out of Him to heal her and that is what happened (Matt. 9:22, Lk 8:46).

If you believe in the power of God and hold steadfastly to it, you will surely obtain it.

Let it be that you have this faith and this feeling in all aspects of your life; in your service, prayer and work.

Even in your fall, believe that there is a power to save you. If you are weaker than the devils, then believe that God who loves you is stronger and that He is able to save you from sin. In strong faith, pray to God to grant you the power you need to succeed in your spiritual life. Ask Him who, *"...always leads us in triumph in Christ..."* (2 Cor. 2:14).

Even if you have been waiting a long time, just believe that the power of God will reach you and save you. This power of God is unseen but it exists and is ready to work with those who ask for it by faith. You need to experience this power which is accompanying you, not only in the life of repentance but in all aspects of your spiritual life so that when you speak, others will feel the strength and the effect of the words you are saying.

The believer is a strong person believing in the power of God working in him.

St. Paul said, *"....to this end I also labour, striving according to His working which works in me mightily...."* (Col. 1:29) and he says about God, *"....to Him who is able to do exceedingly abundantly above all that we ask or think, according to the power that works in us,..."* (Eph. 3:20).

It is faith in the unseen power of God that prompted St. Paul to claim confidently, *"I can do all things through Christ who strengthens me."* (Phil. 4:13).

We ask ourselves; does this phrase only apply to saints like St. Paul? The Lord answers, *"...if you can believe, all things are possible to him who believes..."* (Mark 9:23).

Perhaps this power is a test for our spiritual lives. Do we have faith? Is it a power we are glad of and live in serenity with?

In the church we rejoice in many unseen things.

12. What Happens In Baptism?

Saint Paul says, *"For as many of you as were baptised into Christ have put on Christ."* (Gal. 3:27). How great is this sacrament! Who has seen its promise? Ananias told Saul, *"...and now why are you waiting? Arise and be baptised, and wash away your sins,..."* (Acts 22:16). Who saw these sins being washed away? These are unseen matters which we accept by faith, as the Apostle also said about Christ, *"...He saved us, through the washing of regeneration and renewing of the Holy Spirit..."* (Tit. 3:5). The salvation we obtain by rebirth is an unseen matter but we believe in it according to the Lord's saying, *"He who believes and is baptised will be saved."* (Mark 16:16).

What is the meaning of a second birth? Moreover, what does it mean to be born from above, from God and to be born from water and spirit? The Lord spoke about it in (John 3:3-6). They are all unseen matters; the rebirth from God is an unseen sacrament. We see a person immersed in the baptismal font but we do not see how he is reborn from the spirit. Blessed are those who believe without seeing. The church calls this a sacrament.

The Apostle says, *"....buried with Him in baptism, in which you also were raised with Him through faith..."* and *".... forgiven you all trespass..."* (Col. 2:12). He gives the same meaning in his letter to the Romans and he adds that the old person was crucified with Christ, that we may live with Him (Rom. 6:3-6). Who has seen this death, burial, resurrection, forgiveness of sins, the new life, crucifixion of the old self... these are all unseen matters but we believe in them.

13. The Sacrament of the Holy Eucharist

You see in faith the bread and wine transform into the body and the blood of the Lord. Here you cannot rely on your senses to judge because the bodily senses see only the visible matters. But

the spiritual senses heed to what the Lord says, *"This is my body...*
This is my blood..." (Matt. 26:26, 28), *"Unless you eat the flesh of*
the Son of Man and drink His blood, you have no life in you... My
flesh is food indeed, and My blood is drink indeed. He who eats
My flesh and drinks My blood abides in Me, and I in him." (John
6:53-56).

I do not dispute what the Lord said but I accept it in faith.

In faith we are sure of what we do not see, for what we see is bread
and wine. This is what Saint Paul says, *"The cup of blessing which*
we bless, is it not the communion of the blood of Christ? The
bread which we break, is it not the communion of the body of
Christ?" (1Cor. 10:16) and he also says, *"Therefore whoever eats*
this bread or drinks this cup of the Lord in an unworthy manner
will be guilty of the body and blood of the Lord. For he who eats
and drinks in an unworthy manner eats and drinks judgment to
himself, not discerning the Lord's body." (1 Cor. 11:27, 29).

How can we know if this is the body of the Lord, so as not to gain
judgment upon ourselves? Here, by faith, we go beyond the level
of the senses and the level of the intellect.

Our minds and our senses hinder us from believing the sacraments
of the church. We need the simplicity of faith to believe all what
Jesus Christ and the Apostles said without discussion.

14. To Accept the Sacraments of Christianity

To accept the laying of hands that Barnabas and Saul obtained
from the disciples, so that they could go and serve (Acts 13:2, 3)
and also the laying of Saint Paul's hands on Timothy (2 Tim. 1:6).
We believe that this is a sacrament.

We accept the power the Lord gave in His saying, *"If you forgive* the sins of any, they are forgiven them; if you retain the sins of any, they are retained." (John 20:23); "Whatever you bind on earth will be bound in heaven, and whatever you loose on earth will be loosed in heaven." (Matt. 18:18).

This honour is unseen but we see it through faith. It is not for everyone and no one can take it by himself but he who is called by God, just like Aaron was (Heb. 5:4).

Seeing the unseen is the real spiritual sight. Maybe it is what the Lord meant in His saying to his disciples, "....but blessed are your eyes for they see ...." (Matt. 13:16). What do they see? They see Jesus Christ and His miracles. They see the unseen, like the revelation that St. John saw. Also how Saint Paul saw the third heaven and many other signs (2 Cor.12:2,7).

The Lord rebuked those who did not have this spiritual sense by saying "....and their eyes they have closed, lest they should see with their eyes...." (Matt. 13:15). The Disciple's also wrote the same thing about them (Acts 28:27). The expression 'they closed their eyes', could mean that they did not train themselves to see the spiritual or that they refused to see the spiritual because of their interest in material things.

Gehazi did not see what his teacher Elisha saw (2 Kin 6:17). The companions of Saul did not see anything during the Godly visit, the Bible said that they, "...stood speechless, hearing a voice but seeing no one." (Acts 9:7).

'Faith as small as a mustard seed'

CHAPTER 3

DEGREES AND KINDS OF FAITH

Degrees of Faith

People differ from one another in the kind and degree of faith they have, *"...as God has dealt to each one a measure of faith..."* (Rom. 12:3).

Some may exaggerate by saying that a person with little faith is not at all a believer. This judgment is against the teachings of the Holy Bible, as we will see later. Some may mix between the word 'believer' and 'the chosen', as if these words mean the same thing. Let us then meditate on the different kinds of faith and its degrees.

1. There is the newly converted believer.

The Apostle's ordered that we should be careful not to let this kind of believer be filled with pride or else he will, *"....fall into the same condemnation as the devil."* (1 Titus. 3:6).

2. There are those with little or weak faith.

The following are examples from the Bible about this kind:

• Those who complain about God's care in food or clothes. The Lord gave them an example of the lilies of the field, and that not even Solomon in all his splendour was dressed like one of these. The Lord then rebuked them by saying, *"Now if God so clothes the grass of the field, which today is, and tomorrow is thrown into the oven, will He not much more clothe you, O you of little faith?"* (Matt. 6:28-30, Luke 12:28).

- The Lord also rebuked the disciples, when they thought that they did not take bread with them by saying, *"O you of little faith..."* (Matt. 14:31).

- The Lord rebuked St. Peter when he became afraid after walking with Him on the water and began to sink saying, *"O you of little faith, why did you doubt?"* (Matt. 14:31).

- Similarly, when the disciples were frightened when the waves covered the ship while the Lord was asleep in the stern, the Lord said, *"Why are you fearful, O you of little faith?"* (Matt. 8:26).

Thus fear and doubt in the help of the Lord are evidences of little faith.

- The Apostle gave an example of a person of weak faith who eats only vegetables. The Apostle ordered that one should not judge or mock such a person and said, *"To his own master he stands or falls. Indeed, he will be made to stand, for God is able to make him stand."* (Rom. 14:1-4).

Here I admire the father of the boy who was possessed with an evil spirit, when the Lord asked him, *"Do you believe...?"*, so as to heal his son. The father answered, *"Lord, I believe; help my unbelief!"* (Mark 9:24).

The person with weak faith needs those who pray for him, so that the Lord may help him. We should not mock him for God is able to make him firm in faith.

3. There is a third kind of faith, which is the limited faith.

This person believes in the Lord but only within certain limits and his faith does not exceed these limits. An example of this kind of faith, is Mary and Martha, who believed that the Lord is able to heal their brother from sickness, so as not to die. If he dies however, then their faith was not yet strong enough to believe that he could be raised from dead.

Therefore, each one of them said to the Lord, *"....if You had been here, my brother would not have died."* (John 11:21, 32). When the Lord said to Martha, *"Your brother will rise again,..."*, she answered Him, *"I know that he will rise again in the resurrection at the last day."* (John 11:24). When the Lord went to the tomb and said, *"Take away the stone."*, Martha said, *"Lord, by this time there is a stench, for he has been dead four days..."* (John 11:39).

God did not refuse this limited faith but He gave it a chance to grow. That's why He said to Martha, *"...He who believes in Me, though he may die, he shall live,..."* and He rebuked her at the tomb by saying, *"Did I not say to you that if you would believe you would see the glory of God?"* (John 11:25, 40). He gave her the chance to see the glory of God in raising her brother Lazarus from the dead, so that she believes and also for the Jews who saw the miracle, would also believe.

Here, faith came after the miracle and not before it.

Maybe, it happened like that because this miracle was the first of its kind, namely raising a dead man after four days of being dead and had begun to decay.

4. A fourth kind of weak faith, is the slow heart.

Maybe it comes from a slow understanding, or from lack of comprehension, so the person's faith does not come quickly. This was the kind of faith the disciples of Emmaus had, in respect to the resurrection of the Lord. The Lord rebuked them by saying, *"O foolish ones, and slow of heart to believe in all that the prophets have spoken! Ought not the Christ to have suffered these things..."*

(Luke 24:25-26). He then began to explain to them what was written in all the Scriptures concerning Christ so that they can believe or so that he can cure their lack of faith.

In this example we could also say that it is sound to rectify the misunderstandings concerning the faith. It is much better to rectify than to despise and to mock such people, it won't bring any good and it won't lead to the real faith.

5. There is a dangerous type of faith and that is the dead faith.

St. James the Apostle said, *"...faith by itself, if it does not have works, is dead."* (James 2:17, 20). He also said that this kind of faith cannot save the person (James 2:14) and he also saw that the living faith should have works or deeds to show it, *"...I will show you my faith by my works."* (James 2:18).

6. There is also faith that is not firm.

Jesus explains this lack of firmness in faith when He said to His disciple Peter, *"...Satan has asked for you, that he may sift you as wheat. But I have prayed for you, that your faith should not fail."* (Luke 22:31, 32). Peter's faith did fail but he turned back again and regained his strong faith.

7. There are other cases the Bible describes as deviating from the true faith. The following are examples of this type:

• St. Paul the Apostle said, *"...But if anyone does not provide for his own, and especially for those of his household, he has denied the faith and is worse than an unbeliever."* (1 Tim. 5:8).

• He said about the young widows when their sensual desires overcame their dedication to Christ, *"....they desire to marry, having condemnation because they have cast off their first faith."*

(1 Tim. 5:11,12).

• He also said, *"For the love of money is a root of all kinds of evil, for which some have strayed from the faith in their greediness, and pierced themselves through with many sorrows "* (1 Tim. 6:10).

• He said, *"Guard what was committed to your trust, avoiding the profane and idle babblings and contradictions of what is falsely called knowledge by professing it some have strayed concerning the faith."* (1 Tim. 6:20,21).

In all these examples, can we deny the relationship between faith and deeds?

With a false deed it is said that a person denied the faith, or refused it, or went astray from it, or deviated from it. Maybe with these examples as measures we can examine ourselves, doing what the Apostle said: *"Examine yourselves as to whether you are in the faith."* (2 Cor. 13:5).

8. The most dangerous case is to retreat from faith or lose faith.

The Apostle says, *"In latter times some will depart from the faith, giving heed to deceiving spirits and doctrines of demons..."* (1 Tim. 4:1).

The Apostle speaks about the great falling away that will happen before the coming of Christ, *"....for that day will not come until the rebellion occurs..."* (2 Thes. 2:3).

This is from the general point of view but from the individual point of view the Apostle says, *"Now the just shall live by faith; But if anyone draws back, My soul has no pleasure in him...."* (Heb. 10:38). Here he speaks about the retreat of a believer who was living in faith.

If a believer loses his faith, they are not God's chosen ones, because the chosen ones stay in their faith all their lives until they meet the Lord.

The above are illustrations of negative kinds of faith, let us explain the positive ones.

9. To grow in faith.

St. Paul the Apostle says to the Thessalonians, *"We are bound to thank God always for you, brethren... because your faith grows exceedingly...."* (2 Thes. 1: 3) and he also said to the people of Corinth that their faith increases (2 Cor. 8:7).

Faith is a virtue and like all the other virtues, one can grow in it.

10. To keep the faith and to maintain it.

The Apostle says about himself in his last days, *"I have finished the race, I have kept the faith. Finally, there is laid up for me the crown of righteousness...."* (2 Tim. 4:7-8).

He also says to the Colossians, *"...to present you holy, and blameless in His sight if indeed you continue in the faith, grounded and steadfast, and are not moved away from the hope of the Gospel..."* (Col. 1:23).

11. To be firm in faith.

Saint Peter the apostle says about the devil's wars, *"....resist him, steadfast in the faith...."* (1 Pet. 5:9).

12. To be rich in faith.

Saint James the Apostle says, *"Has God not chosen the poor of this world to be rich in faith and heirs of the kingdom which He promised to those who love Him?"* (James 2:5).

13. To be filled with faith.

It was said about St. Stephen, *"They chose Stephen, a man full of faith and the Holy Spirit...And Stephen, full of faith and power, did great wonders and signs among the people."* (Acts 6:5,8).

14. Faith working with love.

It is said to be indispensable to faith.
St. Paul the Apostle says, *"For in Christ Jesus neither circumcision nor uncircumcision avails anything, but faith working through love,..."* (Gal. 5:6). Maybe he mentioned the expression, 'Working faith' because faith without deeds is dead (James 2:20). The expression 'love' is connected with the whole law and the prophets (Matt.22:40).

15. Faith that performs miracles.

This is a great kind of faith. The Lord spoke about it saying, *"Signs will follow those who believe:" (Mark 16:17)* and St. James the Apostle said, *"...And the prayer of faith will save the sick...."* (James 5:15). The Lord expressed this strongly when He said, *"All things are possible to him who believes."* (Mark 9:23).

16. Faith of confidence and believing.

It is what the Lord used to ask from those who asked for a miracle,

"Do you believe?" He asked the blind man, *"Do you believe that I am able to do this?"* (Matt. 9:28).

The Lord blessed this kind of faith, as when He praised the Canaanite woman, *"Great is your faith!"* (Matt. 15:28) and also to the centurion, *"I have not found such great faith, not even in Israel!"* (Matt. 8:10).

17. The Greatest faith.

Saint Paul the Apostle says, *"...though I have all faith, so that I could move mountains ..."* (1Cor. 13:2). Thus he considered that this faith that moves mountains is the greatest faith, that is its peak and there is none greater than it.

KINDS OF FAITH

There is a great difference between two kinds of faith; Theoretical faith and practical faith.

1. The Theoretical Faith

It is an intellectual or philosophical faith. It is just, the intellectual conviction in the existence of God and in the existence of unseen matters without their influence on life. There is a saying that proves that the devils have this kind of faith. St. James says this about the dead faith, that has no deeds, *"You believe that there is one God. You do well. Even the demons believe and tremble!"* (James 2:19). The book of Job gives us evidence to that point because the conversation between God and Satan proves this theoretical faith. Satan says to the Lord, *"Does Job fear God for nothing? Have You not made a hedge around him, around his household, and around all that he has on every side? You have blessed the work of his hands, and his possessions have increased in the land. But now, stretch out Your hand and touch all that he*

has, and he will surely curse You to Your face!" (Job 1:9-11).
When Satan took permission from God to act, he went to work
against Job. In Satan's second attack, Satan told the Lord,
*"Stretch out Your hand now, and touch his bone and his flesh, and
he will surely curse You to Your face!"* (Job 2:5).

Hence Satan believes theoretically that God exists and that He is
the one who blessed the work of Job and is able to take away what
he has, and to strike his flesh and bones and that any expression
coming out of Job against God is considered a curse towards God.
Despite all of this Satan was fighting the kingdom of God and
God's children and he still does.

The theoretical faith of Satan is a dead faith according to what the
Apostle said, *"...faith without works is dead."* (James 2:20). Thus
if faith without deeds is dead, then what is the faith that has
committed many bad deeds and opposes every goodness.

The theoretical faith is easy. How easy is it to prove the existence
of God with intellectual proofs and the many evidences, the most
important is the practical faith.

This leads us to the important kind of faith.

2. Practical Faith

It is the faith, whose signs show in the practical life, the life of a
believer, believing that God is in front of him, he sees and feels
Him and he acts worthy of this faith.

He loves this God who he believes in His existence, His care and
His protection. He talks to this loving God through his prayers and
his imploring and he fears to do anything that may hurt His loving
heart... and in tranquility in His actions, has no fear and is not
troubled but lives in constant peace. He surrenders his whole life

to God's wise management.

In this way, faith leads the believer to many unaccountable virtues. This kind of faith is the subject of this book, as we will describe how faith leads our whole life to become a fruitful life.

This understanding takes us to another quality of true faith:

3. Perpetual Faith

We mean that faith is not an occasion. Our faith does not only appear when we are in church, or in a spiritual meeting, or when praying, or when reading the Bible, or when having communion; but this faith is apparent at any time and in any place, outside the church as well as inside. God is always in front of us and is always on our minds with faith that does not change. He is not only the Lord of churches or the Lord of the Bible but He is the Lord of the heart and the mind together and the Lord of life.

4. Faith without Seeing

This faith does not depend on the senses and is consistent with what the Lord said, *"Blessed are those who have not seen and yet have believed."* (John 20:29). It is not like the scientists who do not believe in anything unless they test it and convince themselves of it with their eyes and instruments. Also not like the Sadducees who denied the existence of the angels, the resurrection and the spirits (Acts 23:8.) because they could not see them with their eyes.

5. Faith of Confidence From Experience

It is not faith in God, like what we read about in the theological books or in the religious institutions, or in the churches and in the Sunday schools. It is the faith in God that we have experienced and tried in our lives. We were in companionship with Him, we let Him enter in every detail of our lives and practically experienced what David said, *"Oh, taste and see that the Lord is good."* (Ps 34:8). We found that God is wonderful, beyond what we imagined.

Our whole life is a fellowship with Christ. We tasted His beauty, His love and His care; we also saw His power and His glory.

We saw how He enters into our problems and solves them in ways that could not have occurred to us before.

Through our experiences with God we gained confidence in our faith that is not built on information contained in books but on what we felt and have been convinced of and that's why our faith is a true faith firmly established in our hearts.

6. A Strong Faith

It is faith that is able to do anything (Mark 9:23), it can overcome any obstacles, it does not consider that anything is impossible. It was said about Zerubbabel, *"Who are you, O great mountain? Before Zerubbabel you shall become a plain!"* (Zech. 4:7).

It is faith that can step into the water so as to cross the Red Sea in the days of Moses (Ex. 14:22) and to cross the Jordan River in the days of Joshua (Joshua 3). It can walk inside the great sea or river with waters surrounding it like a wall on its right and on its left without any fear.

It is faith that can strike the rock and water comes out of it (Ex. 17:6). It is faith that walks in the desert without any food or guide, collecting its food from the manna descending from heaven day by day (Ex. 16:21), guided by a cloud in the day time and by a pillar of fire at night (Num 9:15-23).

It is the strong faith by which Elijah said, *"There shall not be dew nor rain these years, except at my word."* (1 Kin 17:1) and thus, *"....it would not rain; and it did not rain on the land for three years and six months. And he prayed again and the heaven gave rain"* (James 5:17-18). Elijah had the strong faith that could open and close the heavens.

There are many examples of this strong faith. There are many other examples of this kind but they appear in another form.

7. Faith Which Is Steadfast

It is a steadfast faith and is not at all affected by external circumstances; it believes in God's love either on Mount Carmel or on Golgotha.

We can understand how Abraham believed in the love of God when He gave him descendants from Sarah in hopeless circumstances. But how did Abraham believe in the love of God when He said to him, *"Take now your son, your only son Isaac, whom you love, and go to the land of Moriah...."* (Gen. 22:2)?

Abraham when he raised his hand with the knife to slay his son Isaac, did not doubt in the love of God, nor in His timing. His faith was never shaken in God and not even in the promise that he will have descendants from Isaac, as many as the stars of the sky and the sand of the sea.

Steadfast faith does not change according to the external circumstances surrounding it because its confidence is in God. That steadfast person has peace of heart because they trust in God, His love and the truth that His timing is best.

8. Faith As A Gift

There is another type of faith that is considered a gift from the Holy Spirit and is of a higher degree.

Saint Paul the Apostle, says in his speech about gifts, *"There are diversities of gifts, but the same Spirit. ... But the manifestation of the Spirit is given to each one for the profit of all: for to one is given the word of wisdom through the Spirit, to another the word of knowledge through the same Spirit, to another faith by the same Spirit, to another gifts of healings by the same Spirit,.... "* (1 Cor. 12:4-9).

Faith is also described by St Paul as a fruits of the Spirit. (Gal.5:22). We discover from these verses that we cannot separate faith from works of the Holy Spirit; either from the fruits of the Spirit or from gifts of the Holy Spirit and each of them has its degree.

9. The Sound Faith

How often do people believe in ideas or beliefs whether political or social and their belief gives them a power to carry these ideas out and to transfer them to the minds of the people.

Our aim is to talk about the sound faith that has a spiritual nature and has a deep relationship with God (faith without hypocrisy as was handed down to us by the saints). This faith is pure and refined and should be revealed in our thoughts and behaviour and this leads us to say that faith is not only a belicf but a way of life. Or it is life based on a belief or a belief that people live by and not just ideas found in books.
What we want to speak about in this book is this life, the life of faith.

CHAPTER 4

THE RELATIONSHIP OF FAITH WITH PEACE AND FEARLESSNESS

From the qualities of the believer is that their heart is full of peace and tranquility. They do not get troubled at all, do not get agitated and have no fear because they believe in God's protection. The believer keeps their inner peace whatever the external circumstances are.

The person, who feels that he stands alone, has fear. He who believes that God is with him does not fear. The following are examples:

1. David the prophet.

David said, *"Though an army may encamp against me, My heart shall not fear; Though war should rise against me, In this I will be confident."* (Ps 27:3). If you ask him about the reason for his confidence, he will answer, *"The Lord is the strength of my life; Of whom shall I be afraid?"* (Ps 27:1). David experienced God, His help and His protection. When evil men advanced towards him to devour his flesh he said, *"When the wicked came against me ...They stumbled and fell."* (Ps 27:2).

He does not receive his tranquility because his external circumstances have been improved but he receives his tranquility from God's work in these circumstances and in him.

Consequently David says in the psalm of the shepherd, *"Yea, though I walk through the valley of the shadow of death, I will fear no evil; For You are with me."* (Ps 23:4).

If you have this faith, that God is with you, you shall not fear even if an army besieges you, or if war rises against you, and even if you walk in the valley of the shadow of death.

2. We can also see this peace and fearlessness in the meeting of Elijah the prophet with Ahab.

Ahab the king, was searching for Elijah the prophet everywhere so as to kill him, and in spite of that Elijah went to stand before Ahab. When Obadiah warned Elijah of the danger Elijah answered, *"As the Lord of hosts lives, before whom I stand, I will surely present myself to him today."* (1 Kin 18:15) and the meeting took place. Elijah met Ahab the king and was not afraid of him. Elijah even rebuked him for following the Baals (1 Kin. 18:18). Elijah did not fear because he was confident in his faith that he is standing in front of the Lord.

3. In the same way, we see the encounter between David and the mighty Goliath.

David, the young man, because of his strong faith, was full of peace and did not fear Goliath. He even spoke in confidence and told Saul the king, *"Let no man's heart fail because of him; your servant will go and fight with this Philistine."* (1 Sam. 17:32). As for the king and his whole army they were afraid and very frightened because they were not looking to God who is unseen, as David was. They were concentrating their eyes on what they saw in front of them, 'a champion' who was, *"....six cubits and a span. He had a bronze helmet on his head, and he was armed with a coat of mail, and the weight of the coat was five thousand shekels of bronze."* (1 Sam. 17:4-7).

David, the man of faith, when he entered the field of war let God enter with him and this gave a spirit of faith and peace to the hearts of the men of war with him. The men of war were greatly encouraged to be brave when they heard David say, *"Who is this uncircumcised Philistine, that he should defy the armies of the living God?... Let no man's heart fail because of him; your servant will go and fight with this Philistine"* (1Sam. 17:26,32) and when he told Goliath, *"You come to me with a sword, with a spear, and with a javelin. But I come to you in the name of the Lord of hosts, the God of the armies of Israel..."* (1 Sam. 17:45). What David means is that you come to me with seen matters and I come to you with He who is unseen. We notice that the name of God did not depart from David's lips and this granted him peace.

With this faith, peace of heart and confidence, David advanced towards this Philistine told him with total confidence, *"This day the Lord will deliver you into my hand... for the battle is the Lord's,..."* (1 Sam. 17:46,47).

Truly the person who believes knows no fear, no matter what the circumstances surrounding him are. His peace of heart does not leave him because his faith grants him courage and bravery.

4. In the midst of distress, whatever kind it is, we see faith giving peace.

A distress can be solved in two ways: one is with faith and the other without. A non-believer is troubled, afraid and worried, he imagines the worst results and his thoughts disturb him but the believer accepts it with tranquility and with a wonderful peace of heart. Some may ask him about his feelings regarding this distress and he answers, 'God will interfere in this problem and solve it and it will be for the good'. You may ask him how God will interfere and how God is going to solve it, and he answers: 'I do not know, and I am not interested but I know that we do not have to worry about our problems because God takes care of everything.

Really, I do not know how the problem will be solved but I know

God who will solve it.

Thus, faith leads the believer to tranquility. That's how the children of God always live in peace and even in joy. They feel that God is with them and that He takes care of all their matters and He does for them what they can not do for themselves.

5. Jonah, being in the belly of the whale, did not lose faith and peace.

He even prayed to the Lord when he was in the whale, a prayer full of faith and he said in confidence, *"...I will look again toward Your holy temple."* (Jon. 2:4). He made the Lord a vow and said, *"With the voice of thanksgiving; I will pay what I have vowed. Salvation is of the Lord."* (Jon. 2:9).

Even from inside the whale, he saw the Lord's salvation. He believed that he would get out of the whale, see the holy temple and offer his sacrifice to the Lord and fulfill his vows.

Faith is the source of all peace and comfort. Where there is faith there is no fear and there are no troubles that can overcome us.

6. When faith decreases, then the person fears.

Peter with faith could walk with the Lord on the water forgetting all the laws of gravity. When he remembered them and became afraid, he began to sink. The Lord rebuked him saying, *"O you of little faith, why did you doubt?"* (Matt. 14:31).

Here our Lord showed how fear, doubt and weak faith are related. It is really a wonderful relation: doubt weakens the faith, a weak faith leads to fear and fear causes the fall.

The same thing happened to the Disciples when waves covered the ship and they were sinking. The sight of the agitated waves covering the ship while the Lord was asleep, made them doubt the Lord's care for them. Doubt weakened their faith and so they became frightened, that is why the Lord rebuked them saying, *"Why are you fearful, O you of little faith?"* (Matt. 8:26).

Every time you are afraid, rebuke yourself for your weak faith. Tell yourself, 'where is my faith that God exists and that He controls everyone and sees everything. And where is my faith in God's love, in His helping me in my problems and in His ability to do everything. Where is my faith that God is benevolent and that no doubt He will do me good?'

All these thoughts strengthen your faith and grant you peace and confidence in God's work.

Faith gives rest to the soul because he who believes in the existence of God does not feel lonely but has confidence that there is a power beside him.

He believes in the existence of a Power that is able to do everything. This Power is all love and justice and will support him. This power works for the best of all and has mercy on all who are in distress. If the believer has confidence in this Godly power then his heart is filled with peace and he would not fear or be troubled. The non-believer on the other hand, tires and stands alone in his distress losing his peace because he does not have confidence in this unseen supporting power.

7. St. Peter was in prison and yet he enjoyed a deep sleep.

King Herod, in order to please the Jews, had St. James the brother of St. John, (one from the twelve disciples) put to death. He seized St. Peter also and put him in prison, *"...delivered him to four squads of soldiers to keep him..."* and intended to kill him after the Passover (Acts 12:1-4).

In spite of being in prison, with the strong guards and the expectation of being killed, Peter slept, having confidence in the existence of a Godly guardian that guards him better than the soldiers around him. St Peter slept so deeply that when the angel came to rescue him, he had to strike Peter on the side to wake him up (Acts 12:7).

What kind of peace of heart did he have that let him sleep deeply despite knowing that the next day King Herod was intending to kill him? It is faith in God's care! He had faith that if God wanted him to live he would live or if God wanted him to die as a martyr he would be happy in eternity

In both cases St Peter had no need to be fearful. That is why peace filled his heart. He was sleeping calmly and the external matters did not bother him.

Maybe there was another reason for St. Peter's peace and that is, *"Peter was therefore kept in prison, but constant prayer was offered to God for him by the church."* (Acts 12:5).

The believer is he who can sleep in God's embrace and rest. He surrenders all his life and all his troubles to God, and he says to God: 'As long as you are in control of these matters I will not trouble myself with them. I consider the matter finished as I have transferred them into your hands and I have confidence that You will provide the best outcome. I will sleep in peace and rest for You will give me sleep as David said, *"He gives His beloved sleep..."* (Ps 127:2).'

8. Daniel the prophet and the three saintly youth as an example of faith that provides total peace.

Daniel was waiting to be thrown in the lions' den and in spite of that he did not lose his peace or his courage. He kept his faith and he prayed to God the Lord with strength and without fear.

In the lions' den, Daniel's heart was stronger than the hearts of all the lions that were with him, as if he were saying; 'What if I am thrown into the lion's den? Is not God also there, or is not His angel there who could close up the mouths of the lions?'

Also the three saintly youth did not fear the fire.

No doubt, faith creates great courage and bravery in the heart and it takes away all fear.

9. The saints on their way to martyrdom.

They were singing songs of joy and were praising God on their way to death. Neither death nor suffering troubled them. Their faith was strong in believing in the afterlife, in a happy eternity and in fellowship with God in Paradise. All this filled them with peace and joy and they were even looking forward to death, singing with St. Paul the Apostle, *"...refresh my heart in the Lord..."* (Phil. 20).

Death does not frighten the believer but delights him.

10. In every distress, obstacle and difficulty the believer does not fear and does not lose his peace.

A believer overcomes obstacles without fearing them. He feels that God will solve the problems that he encounters and that God shall not leave him alone in the problems.

Problems for the non-believer on the other hand, cause him to be reluctant and fearful and because of his unbelief he becomes a coward. The non-believer may even imagine difficulties and intimidations that do not exist, as if, *"There is a lion in the road! A lion in the streets!"* (Prov. 26:13).

A believer does not fear at all whatever troubles and difficulties face him. He faces them with calmness and security having confidence in God's work with him.

11. With this faith and reassurance St Athanasius defended against the heresy of Arius.

Despite the political advantages the Arians had and the influence they had on the king and his advisors and the affect this had on the people and the clergy to convince them and cause doubt, St Athanasius stood firm. When they said to him, 'The Whole world is against you Athanasius!', he answered his famous bold statement, 'I am also against the world!'.

St. Athanasius was unmoved despite threats by the Emperors to exile him or threats by Bishops to excommunicate him or the doubts that were everywhere or the false accusations against him. He kept travelling from village to village teaching and convincing the people and removing their doubts and strengthening the true faith of the people. He kept writing articles to respond to the Arian heresy until he was victorious and the faith was victorious through him. St Jerome said, 'There was a time that the world would have been Arian if it wasn't for Athanasius'. St Athanasius faith is not moved by outside influences and knows no fear but maintains his peace even the midst of the fiery furnace until the Lord quenches it.

The faith St Athanasius had in the doctrine he was defending gave him great strength. With this strength of faith he stood against all adversaries and was able to perform great wonders.

12. With faith, people preached about Jesus in countries inhabited by cannibals and they did not fear.

They entered unexplored Africa and entered into the jungles. They encountered dangerous areas from weather conditions, nature and habits of their people and they did not fear. Their belief in God the protector, gave them power and courage. They had boldness also because of their strong faith in the goodness and importance of their work. They believed it was of utmost importance to bring the word of God to the souls there, so that these souls would not perish. God gave them power and took away the fear from their hearts so they accomplished their work. They did not mind the toils of travel, nor the cruelty of the weather, nor the barbarity of the people, nor the difficult weather.

13. By faith, Noah took animals with him on the ark without fear.

God told Noah to take animals with him two by two and he obeyed. God who gave the order, kept Noah safe from them. They were with Noah as they were with Adam in Paradise, who lived with them without fear and with peace of heart.

Noah had faith in God's word to him so he did not fear.

14. He who believes in an idea, their faith in it will give them power to carry it out.

That is why there were reformers in every generation. They believed in an idea and this drove them to carry it out with all their strength. Their faith gave them to endure many troubles until they completed their work.

Gandhi for example, believed in the person's right to freedom and he believed in a policy without violence. This faith gave him a wonderful power with which he liberated India and gave rights to all the people of India whereby they obtained equal rights. He was able to endure so that his followers would not revert to violence and so that they would not oppose violence with violence. His faith in the idea gave him the power to carry it out. How greater it is then to believe in God!

15. Even faith in science does miracles, like the achievements of the astronauts.

I mean by that, that they believed when they were told there was no gravity in space and how a person can walk in this area without falling. Who has the courage to walk in space without having fear? What made the astronauts carry it out was their faith in the scientists' research. Faith gives power and courage. How much more is it then to have faith in God?

The difference between the most courageous people and the most fearful is faith.

The courageous person, is he who has faith that no harm will happen to him, or that he believes in his work and its necessity no matter what he would suffer, or that he believes in the quality of courage and fearlessness. However, the coward is the total opposite of that.

16. Faith in eternity gives a person peace and ease.

He has confidence that he will obtain justice if not on earth then in heaven. This is also how he will obtain his full joy: what has not fulfilled on earth will surely be fulfilled in the eternal paradise. That is how he lives at ease even if he was like poor Lazarus.

17. Faith in the power and the sign of the cross prevents fear.

He who believes in the cross, the sign of the cross, and the power of the cross feels tranquil as he protects himself with it.

If he is faced with fear or danger and he made the sign of the cross his heart will be filled with peace. He will also feel that a power protects him and this power prevents fear from him. He feels that a power has entered his heart which was not there before. The sign of the cross became a weapon for him.

Another person has a great faith in the effectiveness of the psalms. He reads them at any time or in time of need and he feels that the Psalm has a special power that comforts his heart and grants him peace. If he was afraid and read Psalm 91 (he who dwells in the secret place of the Most High), or Psalm 23 (the Lord is my shepherd), or Psalm 27 (the Lord is my light and my salvation) ... he feels immediate peace inside him and that the Psalm's power has descended upon him.

We know that the Psalms were written by inspiration of the Holy Spirit (Matt. 22:43-44). As a book from the Bible, David wrote them lead by the Holy Spirit (2 Pet. 1:21). That is why it has, without any doubt, power.

Others have faith in the spirits of the saints and the work of these spirits for them.

Accordingly, they feel peace when they ask for a prayer or help from a certain saint that they love and they have confidence in the saint's intercession with God.

I remember an Ethiopian monk who was living in a cave in Natroun valley. Once he got lost during the night as he was complaining of weakness in the eyes. Night and darkness fell upon him. So he drew a large circle on the ground and surrounded it with the sign of the cross at all sides and he then slept inside it. In the morning, he saw traces of foxes and animals outside the circle; they could not enter the circle to harm him.

I remember some time ago, I was travelling on a ship. The waves became agitated and the passengers were afraid. I looked and I saw among the passengers, a very good person. I had much confidence in his holiness so my heart was at ease. I said to myself, 'it is impossible that God would allow the ship to sink and this good person, who loves God, is on board'. Sure enough, the ship was rescued and no harm happened. It was just the existence of this person that gave me this peace and strengthened my faith. Maybe, that was also the feeling of other passengers.

There are many uncountable experiences and stories that strengthen the faith but I do not have the capacity to mention them all here.

However what I have mentioned is sufficient for this chapter and now we may introduce another sign of faith.

CHAPTER 5

THE RELATIONSHIP OF FAITH WITH PURITY OF THE HEART

No doubt you are ashamed to sin in front of an innocent person you respect.

You may be very cautious in his presence and are ashamed to commit anything terrible in front of him. You don't want them to have a bad impression of you and think less of you. You even take care not to err in front of any of your servants or the clergy so they don't look at you with contempt, or lessen their respect of you.

Consequently most of your sins are committed in secret either because of fear or shame. It was said about sinners that they, *"...loved darkness rather than light, because their deeds were evil..."* (John 3:19). The Lord said about His enemies who conspired against Him, *"This is your hour, and the power of darkness..."* (Luke 22:53).

If you are ashamed or afraid to sin in front of a person, what should be your attitude if you sin in the presence of God?

If you completely believed that God is present in every place, He sees you, hears you and watches over you, no doubt you will be ashamed or afraid to commit anything wrong in front of Him. That is why, when Joseph the Righteous was tempted to sin, he refused, saying, *"How then can I do this great wickedness, and sin against God?"* (Gen.39:9).

He considered that if he gave in to the temptation he was

committing wrong against God, breaking His commandments and disrespecting Him. Do you have these feelings? Do you place God in front of you in every sin you commit? Do you remember what the Lord said to each of the angels of the seven churches? He told each of them *"I know your deeds."* (Rev. 2:2,9,13,19 and Rev. 3:1,8, 1 5).

If you know this, you will be ashamed and afraid to sin and will struggle to refrain from falling into sin. The fear of God will always be in front of your eyes whenever you try to sin.

You will even feel ashamed from the spirits of the angels and saints.

If you believe, from all your heart, that God's angels roam around us (Ps 34:7) and that we, *"...have been made a spectacle to the world, both to angels and to men..."* (1 Cor.4:9), then you will no doubt be ashamed of yourself from them. He will not bear to see your sins due to his holiness, so he will leave you. You no doubt will be ashamed of yourself from the spirits of the saints, your relatives and acquaintances etc. With this shame you will part from sin and approach the life of purity.

If you believe that God is holy, you will be apprehensive to show your uncleanliness in front of this unlimited holiness. Every time you say 'holy, holy, holy' in your prayers you will feel disgrace in your heart due to your past and you will not venture to commit any sin in the future. When Isaiah the prophet, heard the Seraphim glorify the Lord with this Hymn, "Holy, holy, holy" he cried out, *"Woe is me, for I am undone! Because I am a man of unclean lips..."* (Is 6:2-5).

If you believe that God is the examiner of hearts and reader of minds and that He knows all that goes on in your mind and heart with respect to feelings, plans and desires, then you will be bashful to pollute them. You will be ashamed from His holiness and by stopping or resisting these thoughts and feelings you will reach the life of purity.

Maybe you will say: 'I believe in all these; that God exists, that He sees and hears everything, that He examines hearts and reads minds... and in spite of that I am still in sin.' My answer to you would be that maybe you believe in all these theoretically but you don't live a life suitable to your faith!

He who lives this faith that God sees him, the angels see him, the spirits see him etc., if he practically puts this faith in his heart he will be ashamed to sin, he would not think highly of himself and he will not dare to continue committing sins. According to one of the fathers every sin is preceded by lust, negligence or forgetfulness.

Maybe the person, during sin, forgets God and His kingdom. Maybe he also forgets that he is created in the image and the likeness of God, if he really believed in that. Maybe he is also forgetful of all God's commandments and warnings. Theoretically he believes in all these things but he does not live it. He, as we have already said, has the name of a believer but not the life of one.

Consequently, if you believe in eternity then put it in front of you so as not to err.

He who believes that the day of the Lord will come like a thief (1 Thes. 5:2), that God is just, that He will reward everyone according to his works (Rev. 22:12) and he who believes in life after death, judgment, repentance, punishment, standing before God in that day when the books will be opened, that thoughts and desires will be revealed and the works of everyone will be declared in front of all etc. He who believes in all that, with a practical faith, will find it difficult to err because he will find a restraint inside him which prevents him, fearfully and shamefully. He would be looking forward to meeting God on judgment day.

Why do I speak about Eternity? I could say from another point of view; If you believe in God's love you will be ashamed to hurt His love.

Many times you say, *"God is love"* (1 John 4:8,16). During sin you are not behaving as one who loves God or maybe His love is not at all in your mind. If you really believe that love is the holy bondage that binds you with God, how will you sin? *"Whoever has been born of God does not sin..."* (1 John 3:9).

You will not sin if you believe in virtue as a way of life. Many speak about virtue. They invite others to it and glorify it alot but they do not live virtuous lives. They do not practically believe that virtue can be their way of life. If they practically believed such, they would have lived a pure life and reproved themselves for their weaknesses.

He who also believes that the world is only temporary will renounce it and will not err.

As David the prophet, said, *"I am a stranger in the earth; Do not hide Your commandments from me."* (Ps 11 9:19), *"For I am a stranger with You, A sojourner, as all my fathers were."* (Ps 39:12). That is how the men of faith lived, *"...they were strangers and pilgrims on the earth. ... they desire a better, that is, a heavenly country..."* (Heb. 11:13,16). They renounced everything in this world and obeyed the Apostle's saying, *"Do not love the world or the things in the world..."* And *"...the world is passing away, and the lust of it..."* (1 John 2:15, 17).

With this faith, they lived in the world without the world living in them. They are described as, *"... those who use this world as not misusing it..."* (1 Cor. 7:31). With this faith, yet to a further degree, lived the monks, hermits and the mountain inhabitants in devotion and seclusion, *"...of whom the world was not worthy. They wandered in deserts and mountains, in dens and caves of the earth."* (Heb. 11:38).

This is how faith purifies the heart. As the Apostle said *"And this is the victory that has overcome the world, our fai.th."* (1 John 5:4). Our faith, that we live on earth, *"...while we do not look at the things which are seen, but at the things which are not seen. For the things which are seen are temporary, but the things which are not seen are eternal."* (2 Cor. 4:18). Yes, faith that the world is only temporary lets us overcome it and become purified from it and what it contains.

Faith in eternity makes a person watchful in their conscious. This is how the person will always have a living and beneficial conscious: **to judge every work, not only according to success or failure, or according to its results in our lives... but to judge the matters according to eternity... because everything he does has an effect on his eternal destiny and how it affects the destiny of others.** They are certain that every good they do is kept for them in Heaven and that they will have to give an account of every wrong they do on judgment day.

Faith that God exists and is in front of us gives the heart humility.

It grants the person humility in their heart and in their actions and it grants them fear and reverence because they stand before God. An example is St. Peter when he was fishing after the resurrection of Christ. When he knew that the Lord had come, *"...he put on his outer garment for he had removed it... "* (John 21:7).

In the presence of the Lord, every person stands reverent. According to the person's faith in the presence of God is his measure of reverence. That is how people differ one from the other in their feelings during prayer. There are those who kneel and those who prostrate in front of God's unlimited greatness... but those who sit during prayer, what can I say about them?

The perpetual feeling that God exists - not just during prayer - makes the person humble because majesty is only to God and haughtiness of a person is against faith.

Thus, we see angels in this perpetual reverence.

The Bible says about the Seraphim, *"...each one had six wings: with two he covered his face, with two he covered his feet, and with two he flew."* (Is. 6:2). If the Seraphim covers his face and feet in the presence of God due to His majesty, then what shall we say? To what extent should we be reverent and humble in front of Him?

To this degree we see faith purifying the heart and granting it fear, reverence and humility.

He who believes that God is important to him will fear to sin because sin is separation from God. How dangerous is it for a person to be separated from God!

As for the person who does not believe in the danger of sin and the danger in its spiritual results and becomes lenient with it, they fall into sin and lose their purity. See to what extent the feelings of David were concerning the danger of sin when he told the Lord, *"Against You, You only, have I sinned, And done this evil in Your sight."* (Ps 51:4). See also Joseph, he believed that if he did anyone wrong then it was against God (Gen. 39:9).

All these spiritual feelings either prevent the person from sinning, like Joseph, or they cause a contrite heart, like that of David's. Both are signs of purity of heart.

CHAPTER 6

SIMPLICITY OF FAITH

Many intellectuals seek simplicity of faith but do not find it. Once a philosopher passed by a simple peasant who was kneeling with great reverence and praying passionately. The peasant was talking to God with persistence and familiarity as if he was standing before Him. The philosopher then said; 'I am ready to give up all my philosophy, in return that I may acquire something of the faith of this simple man who talks with all this confidence to Whom he does not see.'

The philosopher felt that this simple man possessed something very precious that all his philosophy he could not obtain.

Simplicity of faith 'believes everything' concerning God and accepts it without requiring evidence or argument; the arguments which the intellectuals are famous for.

This simplicity reminds us of the faith of children who believe in theological and spiritual facts. They have the confidence that does not doubt or lie and does not oppose the mind. Maybe that is one of the reasons that made Jesus tell His disciples, *"Unless you are converted and become as little children, you will by no means enter the kingdom of heaven."* (Matt. 18:3). The faith of an adult may be deeper but the faith of a child is more innocent, simple and sincere; true faith that has no doubts. May your faith be strong like that of a child's.

I do not agree with those who say that children are non- believers. St. Paul the Apostle, tells his disciple Timothy, *"From childhood you have known the Holy Scriptures, which are able to make you wise for salvation through faith which is in Christ Jesus."* (2 Tim. 3:15). How great was the praise of Jesus to the child He set in the middle of the Disciples (Matt. 18:2,3).

He who attains the simplicity of faith, lives far from the complications of the mind and lives far from what the mind presents from doubts, thoughts and misleading's. Really, the mind's balance is from God but it may err if separated from faith.

Faith is a kind of glorious virtue God presents to the mind so as to enlighten it.

If the mind stands alone it troubles its owner with ideas. If David, the young man, depended only on his mind and thoughts, he would have feared Goliath. Saul and his army did but David depended on the simple faith, and he told Goliath, *"This day the Lord will deliver you into my hand..."* (1 Sam. 17:46). However, how would God give Goliath into David's' hands? David did not think of that but left it to God because the war is to God (1 Sam. 17:46). **This is faith**. With it David defeated Goliath and won the war and was more victorious than those who used their minds and tactics.

Simple faith is a matter of confidence and not a matter of thinking.

Even if the mind said that war searches for the balance of powers and how one side will overcome? The answer is simple, if God entered the battle He would change the balance of power and hence David with God's power will be much stronger than Goliath. Here we see that faith - with its simplicity - does not contradict a balanced mind.

He who lives in simple faith lives without anxiety because anxiety usually comes because of much thinking or when a person thinks about problems in an intellectual way. But in the simplicity of faith the person does what he can and leaves the more important points to God Himself and hence he is not anxious. His confidence that God works for him gives him peace of heart and does not allow anxiety to overcome his feelings.

He who has this simple faith is not anxious because he leaves God in control of his matters. If he has confidence in the good care of God in his life, he won't worry about tomorrow, because the God of tomorrow will take care of it and he will welcome everything that happens in his life with the expression, *"...all things work together for good to those who love God..."* (Rom. 8:28).

But he who places his thinking in place of trusting Gods management will become exhausted from his anxieties. Through faith he should let God carry them for him.

The confidence provided by the simple faith that God answers prayers, takes away anxiety.

Maybe you all know the story of this village that suffered from drought. The people of the village decided to set a day for prayer so that God would send rain. All the people went to pray and a young girl went carrying an umbrella. When they asked her about the reason, she said, 'Aren't we praying for rain? What shall we then do when God hears our prayers and it starts to rain and we don't have an umbrella?' She had faith that God will answer their prayer and because of her faith it did rain.

This simple faith is very much needed in regards to miracles and apparitions. A miracle can happen to a person and not to another. The one, in his simple faith, believes and accepts it but the other sees the difficulties that his mind presents and he doubts that a miracle can happen.

The same also happens concerning apparitions. Some see the heavenly apparitions due to their simple faith and others do not due to the complications of their minds. This was illustrated when the Virgin Mary appeared in her church in Zeitoun, Cairo.

The mind tries to analyse everything scientifically or else it will not believe. As for faith, it needs belief, in simplicity, far from the complications of their minds.

That is why miracles and apparitions happen mostly to simple people. Most intellectuals, who disregard miracles and apparitions, mock the believers and it rarely happens that they experience either of them, whether to bring them to faith or so that they are a witness of them (John 15:22).

Even the Jews did not believe the miracle of the man who was born blind and said that he who healed him was a sinner (John 9:24). The mind put the problem of healing on a Sabbath in front of them, so that they lost faith (John 9:16).

That is why Jesus praised the simple people saying, *"I thank You, Father, Lord of heaven and earth, that You have hidden these things from the wise and prudent and have revealed them to babes."* (Matt. 11:25). With the word 'babes', He meant those of simple faith. Those 'wise and learned' in this verse are those who are proud of their knowledge and understanding and who only depend on their minds far from faith. Even some of the spiritual men admitted in sorrow and said: 'This is the fruit which Adam and Eve ate from'. They meant by that, the knowledge away from God.

One night I was returning to the monastery after visiting one of the fathers in the mountain. Darkness was already looming and I remembered that I was told, 'don't come back alone to the monastery so that you don't get lost'. I knew the way quite well and I believed in God's guidance and in spite of that I said, 'If I get lost then I'll spend the night in the desert'. I had strong faith in God's protection, especially that I knew that many Bedouins spend nights in the desert without fear. I was told that I am taking the matter too lightly and that I don't know the mountain. It is full of insects, wild animals and there is also the danger of weather conditions. The mind was telling me to remove what I had in my heart of simple faith ... and I listened to my mind. I came back the same night to the monastery with one of the fathers. On this occasion my mind did not give me the chance to experience the work of God with those who walk at night in the desert, or even to experience the faith of the Bedouin who spends each night there under the care and protection of God.

I thank God that He compensated me for that later on when I lived alone in the mountain.

The mind can imagine danger everywhere and at the same time not consider God's work. On the contrary, it causes the non-believer to be afraid.

That does not mean that a person throws himself in jeopardy without wisdom. If a person was as cautious as can be and then found himself in, so called, 'danger', then with all simplicity he will have confidence in God's protection and care, singing with the prophet David, *"A thousand may fall at your side, And ten thousand at your right hand; But it shall not come near you. "* (Ps 91:7).

Simple faith has confidence that God's hand will interfere to rescue and solve any problem.

The person believes totally that God, as a lover of mankind and benevolent, will no doubt interfere in the problem according to His promises to His children and He will stretch out His hands to solve it.

But how does this happen? Simple faith does not ask that.

He accepts the work of grace in simplicity without investigating how it works.

How many times did we try to solve our problems using human methods and they failed. When the problem is solved we clearly see through faith that it was the finger of God.

Simple faith has confidence in God's work, through belief and experience.

Faith brings the person to trials. Tests deepen the faith and build it on a firm basis and not on theoretical ones. Faith and trials go hand in hand together until the person reaches simplicity of faith.

Simple faith has confidence that everything is possible and that nothing is impossible.

It has complete confidence that God can do all things and that none of His plans can be thwarted (Job 42:2). The person believes in the Lord's saying, *"...all things are possible to him who believes."* (Mark 9:23).

That is why simple faith, overcomes all doubts.

It is a strong faith, stronger than any doubt because doubts are the work of the mind and the mind is proud of its measures but the believer has overcome the stage of the mind and has lived at a higher and deeper level. Higher than doubts is simplicity of faith.

Some try to transfer the problem of religion to philosophy and to bring it out of the heart and the soul and restrict it only to the limit of the mind.

That was what Saint Paul the Apostle fought with all his might, and said. *"...not with wisdom of words, lest the cross of Christ should be made of no effect."* (1 Cor. 1:17-20)

No doubt, the simple believer who gains his faith through experience, above the level of investigation, is stronger in faith than some theologians who acquire their faith from books. They think they have faith. It may be that there faith can be easily shaken by opposing intellectual thoughts.

Train yourself to a life of simple faith and make use of the experiences that happen in your life or the life of others and do not let much thinking keep you far from faith.

CHAPTER 7

OBEDIENCE OF FAITH OR A LIFE OF SUBMISSION

He who believes in God's love, His watching over him, His wisdom, His handling of his life and believes that God is gracious in His acts for him, submits his life to God for Him to plan it as He sees fit. With that conviction, the person will always live in obedience of faith.

He submits his life to God and is tranquil and glad. On the other hand, he who does not live the life of submission is troubled about his life and keeps on thinking: 'What am I? How am I? When am I? Is it necessary that I change what I am doing? Or shall I stay as I am?' Thinking tires him and most probably he loses his peace and continues in a constant search for answers. He discusses the matters with himself without end. He neither thinks of rest nor leaves the matter to God.

The faithful person, when he submits his life to God does not set any conditions on God, does not ask Him for guarantees and does not observe God in His work with him.

He has full confidence in God, in His love, wisdom and ability. He has faith that God knows what is good for him more than he himself does. That is why he submits his life in God's hands and forgets it there.

As long as he has faith in God's work with him, he would not be anxious or concerned and he would not need to tire himself with thinking. The believer lives at peace while he who thinks for himself tires himself.

Many do not submit to God until their human ways fail!

Their normal approach is to completely rely on their human ability, their wisdom, talents and personality. They might tell you that a person turns to God only when they have exhausted all other avenues and it failed. The only time they seek God's intervention is when they have no other option.

This is not faith but it is an urgent necessity for God's help. Faith seeks God in the trivial as well as in the big matters.

Jesus said, *"...for without Me you can do nothing."* (John 15:5). That is because every power we have is from Him, even correct thinking, goodwill and the ability to work. The intelligence on what we depend on is also from Him. How true is the saying of the Apostle, *"...for it is God who works in you both to will and to do for His good pleasure."* (Phil. 2:13).

Our work, in reality, is to participate with God in His work for us. This is our participation with the Godly nature, with the Holy Spirit working in us and for us. Just as St. Paul said about himself and his colleague Apollos, *"For we are God's fellow workers..."* (1 Cor. 3:9).

Every work in which God does not participate in is not a holy or a blessed work. The submission of our will and desire to God is a kind of participation with Him. We are like tools between His hands doing His will. He uses it as He wishes. It works according to His thinking and wishes. By submitting our will to Gods will forms a companionship between us like that between the senses and the brain.

The most dangerous thing that can threaten one's spiritual life is their independence of God.

This is the grave sin that King Saul committed and led to God rejecting him (1 Sam.16). He used to work relying on his own thinking and planning without God's advice and companionship. Saul did not see that he is in need to let God participate with him in the work, as if he was saying: 'As long as I can do this work I'll do it with all power and with all haste, even without prayer because my will alone will carry it out without depending on God. If I fail, then I will seek God! God granted me a mind and a will, so why don't I use them?' There are many like Saul.

God granted humanity the mind and a will but not independent of Him and not so that it would depend upon itself. The Bible says, *"...and lean not on your own understanding."* (Prov. 3:5). We remember that the sin of Adam, the first human, was his attempt to obtain knowledge without God (Genesis 3).

When a person starts to say, 'I know and I can, so what is the use of God in this matter?' He then becomes separated from the faith of God and enters the faith of his ego.

The believer is not only satisfied with dependence on God but also submits everything to Him.

The believer tells Him: 'My life is the work of Your hands and it is now between Your hands, do with it what You want. Where You want me to go I will go and what You want me to be I will be. I do not have a special will, my only wish is that I do Your will and to be one with Your will, to want what You want because You are gracious'.

'I won't behave as though I know what to do. Every human wisdom is foolishness in God's eyes (1 Cor. 1:20). The real wisdom is from You God, alone. You are the wisdom (1 Cor. 1:24). You are, *"...in whom are hidden all the treasures of wisdom and knowledge."* (Col.2:3).'

'I admit that I don't know so I submit my life in Your hands.'

'You know good more than I do and You know the good for me more than I do for myself. I have confidence in Your wisdom and in Your planning for my life. Even if You want me to endure a test or a distress I will accept it from You, knowing that it the best thing for me. Had it not been for Your love for me, You would not have allowed it for me.'

Really, in many cases we don't know where the good is!

The person living the life of submission does not complain or murmur but accepts everything with satisfaction and gladness.

As long as you have confidence in God's wisdom, in His plans for you, then why would you complain or murmur or worry. If complaints or such enter your life, then know that your faith has weakened.

He who lives a life of faith and submission always lives in joy and thankfulness.

The believer does not complain but gives thanks. A smile does not leave his face, cheerfulness does not leave his face and joy does not leave his heart. He believes in God's wisdom and love. He also believes that God's will is always good and useful. He submits to God's will joyfully.

He does not submit to God's will as an obligation or because he is forced to. As if his heart was saying to God; 'what can I do oh Lord? You are strong and I am weak. All what you do I will accept. I am awaiting the end of this matter'. No doubt that these thoughts are of a person who is tired within. He complains that he has no other option but to submit. Submission should not at all be like this.

What is then the meaning of, 'Let your will be done', in the life of faith and submission?

The believer says with all confidence: 'God I submit to your will because I like Your will from the depths of my heart and I have confidence in You and in Your will. Your will has corrected my thoughts, my opinions in certain matters and improved my way of life... how beautiful are your ways Lord, *"How unsearchable are His judgments and His ways past finding out!"* (Rom. 11:33). Your will is the most beautiful song on my tongue and the most beautiful news in my ears. So let your will be done because there is no other will better than it. Next to Your will I am ignorant. When I compare Your will to any other it is far inferior whether it is for me or for others."

The life of submission must be submission with confidence!

We should not submit because of Godly pressure that imposes itself on you and you are obliged to submit to it whether you want it or not. No my brothers and sisters, that is not the meaning of the expression, 'Let Your will be done'. The life of submission teaches us to feel that God's will is truly out of His loving kindness and that it is the best for us and it is a reason for our joy and cheerfulness. That is why David was singing about God's commands, when he tells the Lord that His commands are good for instruction, for pleasure, for meditation etc. (Ps. 119).

Submission to God should be real, not only an outward appearance. Some think that they submit themselves to God when in reality they impose their plans on Him. Every time God acts in his life he tries to stop God and says, 'Wait Lord until I see what You will do. I don't like what You are doing. Instead, do this and that and that will be better for me.' He wants to plan and wants God to fulfill!

Submission is not like that! Submission is to leave God to work, be satisfied with what He does and not to resist God's plans with your actions.

The believer lets God do the planning without interfering or trying to take control.

The sin of Adam was that he began to make decisions independent of God. He decided he wanted to obtain knowledge, to become like God, to build himself... that is why he fell.

The sin of Satan was that he began to manage himself apart from God. He desired to increase and become greater. *"I will ascend into heaven, I will exalt my throne above the stars of God... I will ascend above the heights of the clouds, I will be like the Most High."* (Is 14:13-14). They are plans that resemble daydreaming. Satan planned for himself and he fell.

The same also happened to those who built the tower of Babel. They planned how to build for themselves and they failed. They said, *"Let us build ourselves a city, and a tower whose top is in the heavens; let us make a name for ourselves, lest we be scattered abroad over the face of the whole earth."* (Gen. 11:4). Their planning was their downfall and *"...the Lord scattered them abroad over the face of all the earth."* (Gen. 11:9).

The spiritual person does not do that but submits to God saying, *"Unless the Lord builds the house, They labor in vain who build it."* (Ps. 127:1).

God is he who builds us and not we ourselves, so let us submit ourselves to Him.

That is how we live in peace, having confidence in God's work in us. We stand and observe the miracles from His planning, having confidence that He is gracious and kind and that whatever happens, even if it seems strange or difficult or against what we hoped for, it will be the best.

It is not important if we understand what God does, but that we accept it with faith and submission.

The Bible is full of examples of submission in the lives of the men of faith:

1. Our father Abraham as a example.

Abraham, whose story with God began with God saying to him, *"Get out of your country, From your family And from your father's house, To a land that I will show you."* (Gen. 12:1).

Abraham neither asked why nor where but he just obeyed.

This is the life of submission that does not argue nor discuss, but accepts and obeys without reluctance. It puts its own understanding to the side and concentrates itself on God.

2. That is also how Noah was in the ark, Jonah in the whale's stomach and Moses in the Red Sea. They all had a life of complete submission.

It is the obedience that comes from faith. As long as God wants something then we do not discuss it with Him. What is our limited and weak mind that we discuss with God who is unlimited and full of wisdom? Moses, at the beginning of his message, argued with God on how to go to Pharaoh (Ex. 3) but when he grew in faith and submission he did not argue about entering the Red Sea.

3. St. Mary the Virgins' life is a great example of obedience and submission.

With her love of virginity, she was told to get engaged to a man and to live with him in one house and she obeyed. God sent her an angel to announce that she will be pregnant and give birth to a son and she answered, *"Behold the maidservant of the Lord! Let it be to me according to your word."* (Luke 1:38). She gave birth to Jesus, and saw all the miracles that surrounded the birth, and then was told to escape to Egypt and she accepted all that in obedience of faith. Also in submission she returned from Egypt and accepted to live in Nazareth (Matt. 2:23), about which it was written that nothing good comes from it (John 1:46).

Her motto in this life of submission was her famous saying, *"Let it be to me according to your word."* (Luke 1:38).

4. Faith and submission also appear in the lives of the Apostles.

How they were spontaneous in their obedience to the Lord's call to follow Him.

This is what the Lord told Matthew (Levi) at the tax collector's booth (Mark 2:14). Matthew did not discuss but *"...he left all, rose up, and followed Him."* (Luke 5:28) and did not think at all of his responsibilities and work.

The same also happened when the Lord called Peter, Andrew and the rest of the Apostles. St. Peter summarises their response in his saying to the Lord, *"...we have left all and followed You..."* (Luke 18:28).

It is the obedience that comes from faith that follows God wherever He goes without question, inquiry or thinking about the future. Everyone of these examples obeyed without knowing where they was going (Heb. 11:8).

How many times are we called by God but we stay in our relaxed perception of our future? That's why we ask many questions and try to get guarantees, certainties and security. By this we put aside our faith and hope to attain a secure future that we can see with our eyes or understand with our minds, hence we do not experience the unknown which will be attained only through faith.

5. Jeremiah the prophet, is an example of a life of faith, submission and obedience.

He followed God, in faith, in ways he never thought he would go through and at the end he summarised his experience by his deep saying, *"O Lord, I know the way of man is not in himself; It is not in man who walks to direct his own steps."* (Jer. 10:23). Why doesn't he guide his own steps? Because it is God who leads and guides these steps.

This is the true life of submission, that you walk after God and not your own way.

You walk not according to your wishes and desires and not according to the wishes and/or advice of other people but after God Himself who leads your life. He guides your life to any place and position according to His wisdom. So ask yourself whether God leads your life, or you do, or someone else does.

6. Joseph is a wonderful example of the life of submission.

God showed him a vision that he will reign over his brothers and that they will all bow to him (Gen. 37:10). Yet after the vision what happened? His brothers wanted to kill him but instead threw him in a well and then sold him as a slave to the Ishmaelite's and they sold him to Potiphar to serve in his house (Gen. 37:28).

During all this, Joseph did not murmur against God but kept his peace and submitted calmly to all that God allowed to happen to him. Despite his hardships he was obedient, faithful and sincere. He accepted life as a slave. Although Joseph was content with these misfortunes, his misfortunes kept coming. He was then accused falsely of adultery and thrown in prison as a criminal.

We do not read in the Bible anywhere that Joseph asked God why and where are Your promises? He did not complain.

Joseph is a wonderful example of a life of submission and obedience of faith. The only time he strayed from the life of submission was after explaining a dream to the king's cupbearer when he told him, *"But remember me when it is well with you, and please show kindness to me; make mention of me to Pharaoh, and get me out of this house."* (Gen. 40:14). Yet the Bible tells us, *"Yet the chief butler did not remember Joseph, but forgot him."* (Gen. 40:23). God did not forget Joseph and He got him out to wonderful glory.

7. David the prophet is also an example of one who led a life of submission and obedience of faith.

David was taking care of the sheep in the wilderness. God sent Samuel the king, to anoint David as king. Samuel anointed him but he did not receive the kingdom and kept on caring for the sheep without murmuring. He was then chosen to serve King Saul (who was rejected by God and an evil spirit from the Lord tormented him 1 Sam. 16:14) and David did not complain.

He did not say, 'I am the King chosen by God so how can I serve this rejected person?' In a life of submission he accepted this situation and he used to calm King Saul when the devils tormented him.

Saul then became envious of David and kept hunting him from wilderness to wilderness trying to kill him. Despite this, we do not read that David discussed with God or complained saying, 'where is Your timing? Where is the holy anointing as king? What evil have I done to deserve all this?' But he waited in calmness and submission for the salvation of God and it happened.

8. The Disciples of the Lord are also examples of those who led a life of submission.

The Lord called them for service when He said to Peter and Andrew, *"Follow Me, and I will make you fishers of men."* (Matt. 4:19). Three years passed by and they were still following the Lord without serving. They did not 'fish' anyone. Then the Lord was crucified and they feared and closed themselves in the upper room so that the Jews would not arrest them and in spite of all that they did not complain and remained in the life of faith and submission.

When the Holy Spirit descended on them on the day of Pentecost, the Lord fulfilled His promise. In one day St. Peter saved three thousand souls by one speech. If St. Peter had saved two souls a day during the three years previous, they would be less than the three thousand.

The life of submission teaches the Apostle, *"Wait on the Lord; Be of good courage, And He shall strengthen your heart; Wait, I say, on the Lord!"* (Ps 27:14).

Yes Lord I will wait for Your promise to save souls. But do I have three years to wait, or more? The Divine reply says, *"...it is not for you to know the times or dates the Father has set by His own authority..."* (Acts 1:8).

The life of faith does not question the Lord about His timing.

It does not say to the Lord, 'Why Lord did you make St. Peter wait more than three years to save souls? And why did you let Abraham wait twenty five years so that Your promise would be fulfilled concerning the birth of Isaac? And why did You leave David to be humiliated by Saul ten years until Your promise of becoming a king was fulfilled?'

The life of submission does not doubt and sees that any delay is according to God's wisdom.

David was a young boy when he was chosen. Waiting was beneficial for him while he grew older and matured and also for people's love for him may grow. Waiting was beneficial for St. Peter and the Apostles so that they would complete their discipleship and until the Holy Spirit would descend upon them for them to receive its power. Abraham's waiting for Isaac's birth was beneficial also, so that he would be the son of promise.

9. Of the most beautiful examples of the life of faith is Isaac being presented as a sacrifice.

Abraham was patient for twenty-five years until Isaac was born. Isaac was his beloved son as he was promised by God and Abraham cherished him. When Isaac grew older the Lord told Abraham, *"Take now your son, your only son Isaac, whom you love, and go to the land of Moriah."* (Gen. 22:2). Whose heart could bear this and whose mind can hear that without doubting?

Abraham who led a life of submission did not argue and did not hesitate in carrying it out. He woke up early the next day and took Isaac to sacrifice him. He did not think himself more compassionate than God. He did not doubt at all in God's love and judgment.

Obedience is not relevant only in simple matters but appears in its glory in those matters that seem difficult to carry out.

The true life of submission is revealed when we are asked to enter through the narrow gate and walk the difficult path.

As long as God agrees to allow us to pass through this narrow gate, no doubt it will be the best one to go through. Hence we have not need to discuss the path but enter happily. We know that through this trial God tests the love of His children and the purity of their hearts and prepares crowns for them in His kingdom.

The martyrs endured all kinds of pains and yet were joyful with this kind of faith. All your children Lord, *"Count it all joy when you fall into various trials..."* (James 1:2).

NOT KNOWING WHERE TO GO TO

The following are examples of faithful people who followed God despite not knowing where they would be lead:

1. This is how our **Father Abraham** followed God into the unknown. He did not know where the road will lead him but he had confidence that as long as God accompanied him, He will guide his steps.

2. This is also what happened with the pure **Apostles** when the Lord called them and they followed, without knowing where they were going. At that time, Jesus did not have a known residence and he did not even have a place to rest his head (Luke 9:58). He wandered through the cities and villages teaching and healing despite not having an official profession in the Jewish society. He did have a steady income and when He called His disciples, He even told them, *"Provide neither gold nor silver nor copper in your money belts, nor bag for your journey..."* (Matt. 10:9,10, Mark 6:8).

If one were to have asked one of the Disciples at that time: 'What is your work? What is your future with Christ?' He would not know how to answer except to say that, 'I am living the life of submission.' It suffices him that he walks with Christ even if he is not accomplishing anything.

3. St. Mark the Apostle, when he entered Alexandria.

He entered it without knowing where to go, as there was no church where he could stay. He did not have people to welcome him or give him shelter. On the contrary, idolatry was everywhere and Judaism was opposing the faith. St. Mark came to Egypt with faith and God lead him to Anianos.

What happened to St. Mark happened also to the rest of the Apostles. The names and places may have been different but the heart of the subject is the same. As if every Apostle was saying, 'If the service was a human work it would interest me to plan my way; but if the service is a Godly work, I don't care where I go as I am with God.'

4. John the Baptist saw that his duty was to witness the truth. He witnessed the truth and rebuked King Herod without fearing whether it would lead to prison or to death. The message of God was conveyed in complete obedience of faith. Life and destiny are submitted to God to fulfill.

This was how St. Paul witnessed for the Lord without caring if he got into, *"...tribulation, or distress, or persecution, or famine, or nakedness, or peril, or sword?"* (Rom. 8:35). He says with confidence having the life of submission, *"...in all these things we are more than conquerors through Him who loved us."* (Rom. 8:37).

In all these matters, the children of God walked the life of submission.

All that interested them was for God to lead them and they did not care where to. They have confidence in faith, that they will be lead to green pastures and to wells of living water. Their experience with God made them happy to be guided by Him and they had confidence in His love.

5. Isaac the son of Abraham carried wood on his back thinking it was for an offering for the Lord and he went with his father, not knowing where were going. All Isaac learned in his life was submission and obedience and so he went to be sacrificed. Abraham tied him up and put him on the altar on top of the wood (Gen. 22) and raised his knife. All this done and Isaac was in complete submission. He did not doubt in his father's love nor in the love of God and the result was that he always prospered.

With his submission, he gained his life, the obedience of faith and God's promises.

6. The servant of Abraham, when he went out to search for a wife for Isaac, not knowing where to go.

He submitted his path to the guidance of God. God planned everything for him in a wonderful way that astonished him. Everything happened according to what Abraham asked him and that's why he said, *"...the Lord has prospered my way..."* (Gen 24:56).

As if he was saying, 'I did not know where I was going but I knew that God would be with me'

Also Jacob on his journey to his uncle Laban had a similar experience. How beautiful is the Lord's saying to him, *"I am with you and will keep you wherever you go."* (Gen. 28:15).

7. The Israelites in the wilderness did not know where they were going.

They did not know anything. God used to guide them day by day. They would go or stay according to God's guidance. This guidance was in the form of a cloud during the day and a pillar of fire in the night. The people were in complete submission to God's guidance without questioning.

Moses did not have a plan for his journey nor a map to follow. It was as if he was saying, 'It is enough for me Lord that Your cloud is above our heads and the pillar of fire in front of us. We do not plan our way but Your good will does. We are happy to be under Your guidance. Wherever Your cloud goes we will also go and wherever it stays we will stay under it.' Let the tabernacle in the wilderness move towards the unknown. It is unknown to us but not to You. You have planned this journey since the beginning of time. This knowledge of Your care is sufficient for us to submit to the unknown and we have complete confidence that we are on the way to Canaan'.

8. St. Anthony, the father of monks, when he entered the desert did not know where he was going. Also St. Paul the first of the hermits and all the other saints and hermits, when they entered the unknown wilderness they did not have a certain place in mind to go to. What was in front of them was the spiritual aim: To be alone with God in a calm and peaceful life, submitting their lives totally to Him, '...wandering in the wilderness, mountains and the caves of the earth'.

If you ask any of the hermits where they are staying, they would answer, 'On a map. I do not know where this place is that I live but on the map of love I know that I am in the Father's embrace.'

Some may ask: 'Shouldn't everyone plan their way, as the Lord commanded.' (Luke 14:28)?

The life of faith is far from the science of mathematics. So then what does Saint Luke mean when he wrote that everyone should sit down and count the cost?

The cost we need to count is Do we have enough faith?

Do you have enough faith for you to submit the whole matter for God to manage it? You do what you can but the principal point is your faith in what God does and your submitting to Him the whole matter.

This is our way when we wanted to build a church or any project for service or caring. The main question was not, 'From where do we get the money?' but the main question is, 'Does God agree with this project or not?' If He allows it then He will take care of the costs, we only have to start it and God's hand completes the work with us; *"Unless the Lord builds the house, They labour in vain who build it."* (Ps 127:1).

Faith is that you close your eyes and look to God.

As long as you open your eyes you will walk with the bodily senses but if you close this bodily eye you will walk with heart and soul.

If you are convinced with your spiritual senses that God will go with you on your path, walk in it even if it was through the valley of the shadow of death, having confidence that there you will not fear any evil because God is with you (Psalm 23).

This is the life of submission, where God chooses for us what we want, not us choosing for ourselves. We need to learn from the story of Lot and Abraham.

Lot chose for himself to live in Sodom and he knew where he was going to. Abraham did not choose anything for himself but God told him, *"Get out of your country, From your family And from your father's house, To a land that I will show you."* (Gen. 12:1) and what was the result? Lot was cursed when he was in Sodom and became a captive of war till Abraham saved him (Gen. 14). All that he owned was burnt and he lost everything there. Abraham on the other hand, lived in submission to God and was successful.

CHAPTER 8

WHAT STRENGTHENS FAITH?

Faith is a virtue like all other virtues; it can be strengthened and it can be weakened.

We should not only have faith but pursue all the means that make it grow and increase (2 Thess.1:3 & 2 Cor.8:7). What are the means that strengthen our faith?

1. Confidence In God's Qualities

- Always put in your heart that God is gracious and compassionate. By reminding yourself of this, you will strengthen your faith in His care and protection. Always remind yourself that, *"...all things work together for good to those who love God..."* (Rom. 8:28). Have confidence that everything God does is out of love for you and that everything He allows to happen will no doubt lead to good no matter what it is. God was gracious to Joseph when he was sold as a slave and falsely thrown into prison. All these distresses were in God's plan for the good of Joseph and for the good of the whole region. This is what Joseph told his brothers, *"So now it was not you who sent me here, but God;..."* (Gen. 45:8), *"...you meant evil against me; but God meant it for good, in order to bring it about as it is this day..."* (Gen. 50:20).

- Have confidence that God is a father and that He is the Living One. No doubt, He treats His children with tenderness and gives them good gifts. God said, in His fatherly tenderness, that He engraved us on the palms of His hands (Is 49:16). Even if a mother forgot her child, He won't forget us (Is 49:15). In His fatherhood He gives us all that we need without asking.

- What also strengthens faith is to have confidence in God's ability to do anything. He loves you and wants what's best for you. He has the ability to do anything and nothing is impossible for Him.

  When our father Abraham raised the knife to sacrifice his only son Isaac, he had faith that God is loving and He knows what is best. According to God's promise Abraham had full faith that he will have as many descendants from Isaac as the stars of the sky.

  He even had faith that if Isaac died God was able to raise him from the dead and to fulfill His promise, *"...that God was able to raise him up, even from the dead..."* (Heb. 11:19). Abraham believed that he would be, *"...a father of many nations in the presence of Him whom he believed - God, who gives life to the dead and calls those things which do not exist as though they did;"* (Rom. 4:17).

  Moses entered the Red Sea and crossed it having faith in God's ability to do anything and Joshua entered the Jordan River and also crossed it; each one of them with his people.

- Have confidence in God's judgment and that all His planning is for good, even if you don't understand the depth of His judgment.

  If you believe in God's judgment, you will live in peace and accept everything with satisfaction but if your human mind doesn't have confidence in God's judgment, you will lose your peace, complain and be anxious. No matter what happens to you, you should say to God, 'I have confidence Lord in Your judgment and in Your good planning and I know that later I will understand what You were doing, just like Joseph did.' Have confidence, that God is gracious, that He is a loving father, that

He is wise in His planning, that He wants good for you and that He is able. All these things deepen your faith and grant you peace of heart.

2. Confidence in God's timing

God promised our father Abram that He will give him descendants and He did grant him many descendants, although it took a long time. The Lord promised him that his descendants will be as numerous as the stars of the sky, even though his wife was barren and he was of old age and eventually the promise was fulfilled. God also promised His people freedom from captivity and He did free them. He promised Elijah to help him in the time of famine and He did aid him with a miracle (1 Kin 17:3-6).

God promised our mother Eve that her descendants will crush the head of the serpent (Gen. 3:15); this promise was fulfilled on the cross.

God also promised that He would pour out His Spirit on all people (Joel 2:28) and He did that on the day of Pentecost and His Spirit is still dwelling in us and we are a temple for it (1 Cor. 3:16).

All God's promises are sincere. We need God's promises as much as those, long ago in history, did.

They are everlasting promises from God. They comfort us when we live in them and in faith. For example, the Lord's saying, *"...I am with you always, even to the end of the age."* (Matt. 28:20), *"For where two or three are gathered together in My name, I am there in the midst of them."* (Matt. 18:20), *"I will give you a mouth and wisdom which all your adversaries will not be able to contradict or resist."* (Luke 21:15), *"Do not worry about how or what you should speak. For it will be given to you in that hour what you should speak; for it is not you who speak, but the Spirit of your Father who speaks in you."* (Matt. 10:19-20), also His saying about the church, that the gates of Hell will not overcome it (Matt. 16:18).

May we live in these promises with all our hearts, so as to strengthen our faith.

How wonderful it would be if you, dear reader, collect all these promises and read them frequently. No doubt you would feel that God is sincere in His promises and consequently would live happily with peace and comfort. The continuous remembrance of God's promises comforts the soul and strengthens the faith.

3. Look Unto God And Not Unto The Surrounding Circumstances

The surrounding circumstances looked hopeless before the children of Israel at the Red Sea but Moses called the people to look unto God and said to them, *"Stand still, and see the salvation of the Lord, which He will accomplish for you ... The Lord will fight for you, and you shall hold your peace."* (Ex 14:13-14).

The same also happened to David and the mighty Goliath. If David looked to the mighty and challenging Goliath he would have been at a loss but through faith he looked unto God who could deliver him into his hand (1 Sam. 17).

The same situation also happened in the miracle of the five loaves and the two fish. When the disciples saw the food that was available and the thousands of people present they said, *"... but what are they among so many?"* (John 6:9), but Jesus looked up and blessed the food. If the disciples also looked up with faith they would have had confidence and seen the power of God.

Martha looked at the tomb of her dead brother, who had been dead for four days and exclaimed that by now there would be a stench. But the Lord said to her, *"Did I not say to you that if you would believe you would see the glory of God?"* (John 11:39-40).

So we always have to look to God above so that faith enters our hearts.

We have to look up unto the loving God who is able to do anything and not to concentrate our thoughts on the surrounding circumstances.

Do not look to the power of your enemies but look unto God who will rescue you from them.

Do not look at the sin which, *"...has cast down many wounded, And all who were slain by her were strong men.."* (Prov. 7:26) but look unto the Lord Jesus who, *"...will save His people from their sins."* (Matt. 1:21).

4. Stories of Faith and Contemplation On the Lives of the Men of Faith.

That's why when God wanted to give lessons about faith He said, *"Consider the lilies of the field... even Solomon in all his glory was not arrayed like one of these. Now if God so clothes the grass of the field, which today is, and tomorrow is thrown into the oven, will He not much more clothe you, O you of little faith?"* (Matt. 6:28-29).

He also said, *"Look at the birds of the air,...."* (Matt. 6:26). Once I did what the Lord ordered and I looked at a bird in the garden of the monastery. It had many grains in front of it and yet it only picked up two or three, left all the rest and flew away. It did not store them in a barn. It had confidence that in any place it flies to, the Lord will grant it food, so why should it store grains? Why should it leave the high and the wide sky to stay near the grains to store them, like the ants do.

The Lord gave us a similar example in the story of the manna which

He sent from heaven.

The people were instructed to collect it according to their needs day by day without storing it. Those who didn't obey and stored it, discovered that the manna became rotten with *"...worms and stank."* (Ex. 16:20).

Whenever a person reads stories of people with great faith, about their confidence in God and the miracles that happened to them, his heart will be filled with faith and he will come to love this life of great faith. Also when you associate with men of faith, you will learn to imitate their live. God's work in their lives will encourage you and inspire you to take them as an example. That is why one of the fathers said, 'The recollection of the lives of the saints is nourishing'. For this reason, the Bible has many stories of faith for us to learn from. It will also strengthen our faith, as we see practical examples of the life of faith. We see in front of us the path the men of faith travelled and how God treated them and how they dealt with Him.

If reading affects a person then there is no doubt, their association with someone of faith will have a deeper effect. So associate with those who have faith and absorb the faith from them. A person acquires faith by submission more than by learning. Look how they live, how faith appears in their lives, how they deal with God and how they react towards certain circumstances. No doubt if you do this your faith will be strengthened.

5.Humility Of Heart And Mind.

The humble person is content to accept all that comes from God but the mind that is proud discusses, argues and refuses what doesn't please it and hence cannot attain the faith of a humble person.

The humble person admits that his mind is limited and that his abilities are limited and that he cannot comprehend God, the unlimited. He does not perceive the depths of God's wisdom and abilities and so he is able to accepts in faith and without doubt. If his mind becomes anxious, he would then lay down before God and say, 'Your ways O Lord are above my understanding and Your works are above my knowledge. Who am I in front of You? All my knowledge is ignorance in front of You'.

We should receive from God through submission and not from inspection. Give me O Lord the faith of children and not that of the philosophers or wise men (Luke 10:21).

Should we study the story of the three saintly youth in the fiery furnace (Dan. 3:25) with our limited understanding or should we accept it in faith with a humble mind that bows down before the miracle? The miracle is the work of God who is able to do anything.

Faith needs the humility of the mind and the simplicity of the heart and it also needs:-

6. Experiences With God

Try and submit your life to God, live with Him and test Him, try to rely on Him and then you will see His miracles working with you. If however you limit yourself to your own abilities, human wisdom, the experiences of society, people's advice away from God etc. then you are eating every day from the tree of knowledge and you will never develop your faith? Therefore, test practically the existence of God in your life. Associate with Him so that you know who He is and as David the prophet said, *"Oh, taste and see that the Lord is good."* (Ps 34:8).

So how can we experience God? By the following:

7. See God In Every Matter.

People's faith does not grow stronger when they live in a world separated from God. They give reasons to things that happen in this world without mentioning the name of God, as if the world rotates without Him.

As an example: Man can split an atom, use nuclear energy, build space-crafts, reach the moon, travel the universe and work with electronics etc.. People then praise how great the human mind is, or how great is the nation that invented all those things! These people fail to mention God's name in all these things!

The believer on the other hand glorifies God, the creator of this human mind. They know that God granted him talent and ability to do these works and He revealed to him all the power in nature. If believers know all this, then what can they say about God Himself who is unlimited and can do anything? What strengthens the faith of the believer is that he relates every power and every miracle to God.

Another example: A person gets sick with a fatal illness and a doctor saves him from death and he is healed. The sick person and his family admire the cleverness of the doctor, so they thank him in the newspapers and praise him, and consider him the cause for the healing. The name of God is never uttered on their lips.

The believer would instead thank God that He healed the sick person, that His hand was with the doctor's hand.

A third example: A person is subjected to an accident that would have cost him his life, had there not been a driver who stopped the car a few centimeters from him. The people shout and comment how skillful the driver is but the believer knows that God granted this person a new life. How beautiful it would be if you search for God's hand in every incident so as to strengthen your faith.

Search for God's judgments and work them into your daily life. In this manner you will find God every day, you will touch and deal with Him and you feel His presence in everything that happens to you, whether it is small or big. In this way your faith will increase day by day.

A fourth example: If a believer passes by a garden and sees a flower it would not be suffice to enjoy its shape and smell, as an intellectual would do, but he would stand overwhelmed in front of it contemplating on the beauty of God's creation. What wonderful colours these are that no artist, no matter how talented they were, could recreate. Artificial flowers are accurate and beautiful but are not so precisely arranged and they have no life to emanate or any aroma. It is dead beauty.

Truly, contemplating on nature like this strengthens faith.

All people throughout the world admire nature, yet most of them separated it from God. However, he, who wants to strengthen his faith, sees God in nature. Isn't it His creation? This is what David the prophet said, *"The heavens declare the glory of God; And the firmament shows His handiwork."* (Ps 19:1). Do you admire a moonlit night without glorifying God the creator of the moon? Remember God in this way so that He becomes a practical reality to you and not just an intellectual reality to be proved with evidences. In this way you will live with God every day.

If you desire to strengthen your faith then don't separate God's creations from Him.

Do not be in awe of nature and forget God. Don't be in awe of human intelligence and its achievements but say, 'You are wonderful Lord! How did you create the material world like this with its characteristics and properties for man to use for his own means.'

Do we wonder about a scientist who extracts a medicine from a certain material, whereas we forget God who put this property in this material so that it can serve the medical aim!

Another way that you can strengthen your faith is:

8.Take The Lord As Your Friend

If you did this, it would strengthen your faith because you will build a relationship with God and talk with Him without fear.

Many look unto God as a lord or master. But did you look unto Him as a loving friend, having confidence in Him and in His loyalty. He knocks at your door and asks you to open the door as a friend. He will enter and eat with you and you with Him (Rev. 3:20). If you accepted God's friendship and love, you will gain true, deep faith. You will look forward to talking to Him as a friend, to tell Him your secrets and enjoy His companionship and love. Because He is your friend, you will take care not to hurt His feelings or disrespect Him. He, Himself, will reveal His secrets to you as He did with Abraham (Gen. 18:17).

God wants this type of relationship with you as He said, *"No longer do I call you servants... but I have called you friends."* (John 15:15). So take Him then as a friend or Father, believe in His sovereignty and power and share your secrets with Him and He will share His with you.

From the stories of friendship with God is Elijah the prophet. Their relationship is well illustrated when God instructed Elijah to anoint Elisha as a prophet after him.

One day the Lord told Elijah, the great prophet, *"...anoint Jehu the son of Nimshi as king over Israel. And Elisha the son of Shaphat of Abel Meholah you shall anoint as prophet in your place."* (1 Kin

19:16).

Elijah did not say; 'Well, Lord I will anoint Jehua a king, but how can I anoint a prophet in my place? Are you not in need of my services? Does this happen now after my great efforts for your sake and after standing before King Ahab and his wife Jezebel and after freeing the land from all the prophets of Baal? Has Your love for me changed?'

Elijah did not say anything of the sort and did not doubt in God's love but did what God ordered, having confidence in God's love and wisdom. Elijah considered it familiarity and friendship with God. God made Elijah participate with Him in carrying out the Godly plan, even if he had to anoint a prophet in his place. This does not mean that the friendship between him and God had ended or was diminished. The proof is that God raised him, later on, in glory to Him in heaven (2 Kin 2:11) and He also appeared and talked with him on Mount Carmel. It is love that God made clear to him even in the matters concerning him. The anointment of a prophet in his place was the beginning of his promotion to a state greater than that of a prophet.

9. Prayer For The Sake Of Faith

Pray for your faith that it may grow and increase.

Tell Him; 'Give me O Lord, that I believe in You with full faith. Give me that I love and have confidence in You in everything and to believe that You are gracious and compassionate, even if the world seems dark to me. Let me feel that my mind is too limited to understand Your wisdom and judgments. I know that You are the gracious Lord and the provider of all good things, that You are loving, that You see everything and that You are capable of doing everything and in spite of that my faith often weakens... so help my weak faith.

CHAPTER 9

WHAT WEAKENS FAITH

The devil labours continuously with all his efforts to weaken the believers' faith. He and his companions try to deceive even the elect (Matt. 24:24). It does not suffice them only to weaken the faith, but even to turn their victim into an unbeliever. At the end of the days many will abandon the faith, *"...giving heed to deceiving spirits and doctrines of demons..."* (1 Tim. 4:1) from the devils' deceit. How fearful is the Lord Jesus saying about His Second Coming, *"Nevertheless, when the Son of Man comes, will He really find faith on the earth?"* (Luke 18:8).

What are the demon's tricks to weaken our faith? There are many - some are strong and aggressive while others are sly and difficult to detect.

1. The Ego.

Our ego often opposes and refuses God because He commands against its sinful desires.

The ego feels that God limits its freedom. It desires things God does not agree upon and wants to enjoy this liberty or this negligence and so it separates itself from God, as the prodigal son did. He left his father's house (Luke 15:11-14) to spend his share of the money as he wished ... or in other words he refused God. The unbelievers are examples of those who refuse God and their motto becomes; 'It is good that God does not exist, so that I can exist.'

These people have misunderstood the real meaning of existence and the real meaning of freedom. Liberty is not doing what one wishes because our wishes may be wrong. The true liberty is to be freed from all that captivates them! To be freed from bad habits that enslave them, from the sinful desires that defiles them, to be freed from the supremacy of material things in their lives etc., freedom from all that prevents us from soaring towards God and from companionship with God. This is the true meaning of our existence.

Our ego hinders our faith; as we desire power, greatness and pride, we tend to see God as a rival to our heart and soul

Herod the king found that the new born Messiah in Bethlehem will share with him his reign. He refused to accept this and tried to get rid of the baby Jesus, the Christ, by killing Him. The Pharisees are also examples like Herod, who saw Jesus taking their place and gaining respect as a teacher. They said to each other, *"You see that you are accomplishing nothing. Look, the world has gone after Him!"* (John 12:19).

Many refused to believe in Jesus Christ's resurrection because of their ego. They thought that to deny the resurrection meant that they would be innocent of Jesus blood (Acts 5:28) The ego is the greatest hindrance to faith. Accordingly, the Lord said, *"If anyone desires to come after Me, let him deny himself... "* (Matt. 16:24). He also said, *"He who finds his life will lose it, and he who loses his life for My sake will find it."* (Matt. 10:39). Thus, St. Paul the Apostle says concerning faith, *"... nor do I count my life dear to myself, so that I may finish my race... "* (Acts 20:24), *"I also count all things loss for the excellence of the knowledge of Christ Jesus my Lord, for whom I have suffered the loss of all things, and count them as rubbish, that I may gain Christ and be found in Him."* (Phil. 3:8-9). Do you feel like St. Paul? or...

Is your faith hindered due to your ego, your wishes, your desires, your ideas and your passions?

Is there opposition between God and your ego? If there is then deny yourself, resist it, overcome it because better is a man who controls his soul than one who controls a city (Prov. 16:32).

The Pharisees, scribes and priests took much care of their ego. In each of them there were faults. When Jesus gave sermons to the crowds they were convicted of their faults. For this reason they hated Him and didn't believe in Him because He was the Light that revealed their darkness. Their egos' were obstacles to their faith.

We call to mind that the devil's ego was the main reason for his losing his faith and being cast out of Heaven.

When the devil thought how to magnify himself, how to ascend to Heaven, place his chair above God's and become like the Most High (Is 14:14), he opposed God. He put his faith in himself and not in God. As for the virtuous angels, they kept their places because in their faith in God, they considered themselves, *"...His hosts,...ministers of His, who do His pleasure."* (Ps 103:21).

Many find themselves beautiful in their own eyes, they worship themselves like an idol.

What prevents them from the life of faith is the love of self, self-esteem, the desire to magnify oneself, to fulfill selfish passions and to run away from everything that reveals faults in it. They want to live in an atmosphere of self righteousness and praise. They are annoyed from every sincere word, every reproach and every punishment. So how can they live in faith?

If you are like this, try to improve yourself so that you humble yourself before God and live in faith.

From the attributes that also weaken faith:

2. Reliance/Dependence On The Senses.

This is what happened to St. Thomas the Apostle, when he refused to believe in the resurrection of the Lord and said, *"Unless I see in His hands the print of the nails, and put my finger into the print of the nails, and put my hand into His side, I will not believe."* (John 20:25). God sympathised with the weakness of Thomas's faith and permitted him to become sure through his senses by saying, *"...stop doubting and believe..."* (John 20:27) and then He rebuked him saying, *"Because you have seen Me, you have believed. Blessed are those who have not seen and yet have believed."* (John 20:29). What the person sees we call observation and not faith but it may lead to faith.

If this faith is weak, there is an even weaker faith and that is he who sees and still does not believe. As an example of those are the priests who saw the empty tomb and did not believe in the resurrection. The Pharisees who saw the miracles of Jesus, like the healing of the man born blind and the people whom Jesus raised from the dead and yet they still did not believe. They refused faith due to reasons in their hearts. What our father Abraham said to Lazarus applies to them, *"...neither will they be persuaded though one rise from the dead."* (Luke 16:31).

3. Submitting Faith To The Mind

The mind has limits which cannot be overcome and faith is a higher level than that. But there are people who want their minds to perceive the unlimited, the miracles and what is beyond their understanding or else, they refuse all this!

They want to submit the theological power to scientific research which is logically impossible. Hence, it can be concluded that it is not reasonable for the limited human mind to subdue the unlimited.

Maybe as an example of this, is what is known today as the 'New

Theology'. In some of the institutes, they want to submit the soul and miracles to pure scientific research or to symbolic explanations. Thus they deny many of the miracles and many stories told in the Bible and mix it with mythology! Truly the soul is lost if it tries to think too highly of its minds capabilities (Rom. 12:3). These people diminish their faith and try to lead others astray as well.

4. Associating With People of Weak Faith (Doubters):

Just as the company of faithful men strengthens faith, the company of doubtful men plants doubt in the hearts and minds of others. These doubts may grow due to their persistence or because the doubts are convincing. His doubts would grow because his level of knowledge and intellect are less than the person he associates with. Or simply because his faith was shallow.

For this reason the Bible speaks strongly against association with heretics.

Saint John, the apostle, says, *"If anyone comes to you and does not bring this doctrine, do not receive him into your house nor greet him; for he who greets him shares in his evil deeds.. "* (2 John 1:10). That is why the church prevented association with the heretics and the excommunicated.

How many people associate with non-Christian groups like the Jehovah's witnesses for example and the result is that they lose their direction. How many church members associated with foreign groups or heretics and their beliefs where deeply affected.

Being easily influenced by people who have doubts in their faith can weaken your faith. You may be faced with a trial or a problem and you may accept it in faith, submitting the matter to God and thanking Him for everything. Then, a person with little faith visits you and he keeps on explaining how dangerous the matter is and frightens you of its results until you lose your peace of heart. It also weakens your faith in God's care and you get worried.

Be careful with whom you associate and with whom you share your experiences and trials.

This leads us to another point which also weakens faith:

5. Being Easily Influenced And Having A Weak Personality:

Mary Magdalene is as an example of this type. She saw the empty tomb, heard the angel's good news, even saw the Lord Jesus after His resurrection, held onto His feet, heard His voice, and He gave her a message... but after all that she said three times, *"They have taken away the Lord out of the tomb, and we do not know where they have laid Him."* (John 20:2,3,13,15). Hence she ended up denying the resurrection. What caused this doubt? and how did her faith weaken after seeing Jesus and speaking with Him (Mark 16:9, Matt. 28:9)?

Mary Magdalene was young in age. Her belief weakened due to the rumors which the Jewish priests spread against the resurrection. She also weakened due to the Disciples' disbelief in the resurrection (Mark 16:11,13,14). Doubts and suspicions entered her heart and then she repeated the doubtful rumours that she heard.

The faith of Mary Magdalene could not oppose the rumours and people's doubts. She was inwardly moved due to the outer pressure and she yielded to it.

Many people are inwardly moved. They retreat from their first faith, belief or behaviour, due to people's mockery. As a result their personality is weaker than the opposition.

God wants your personalities to be strong. As the Apostle says, *"Always be ready to give a defense to everyone who asks you a reason for the hope that is in you.* " (1 Peter 3:15). Children of God are not weak. They should not be like those whose faith, or rather spiritualties, are moved or yield to any outer ideas. They should apply what the Apostle says, *"Therefore, my beloved brethren, be steadfast, immovable... "* (1 Cor. 15:58).

Our mother Eve is also an example of the kind who deviated from faith by being easily influenced. The snake deceived her by putting doubts into her mind and it resulted in her being sent out of Paradise.

How many go after rumours and believe them. How many utter words about the Second Coming and people believe them. They say the Anti-Christ is born, is in an American State and that he is now 17 years of age!! And also that the world will come to an end on a certain date! How many dates did the Jehovah's Witnesses fix about the second coming and none of them were true.

The faith of some may weaken and cause them to following those who claim they saw visions or dreams.

They believe in those who claim to have visions and dreams from God! They are deceived by what these people say, even if it was against their beliefs and spiritual principles. Since the days of Moses, God warned against these people saying, *"If there arises among you a prophet or a dreamer of dreams, and he gives you a sign or a wonder, and the sign or the wonder comes to pass, of which he spoke to you, saying, `Let us go after other gods'--which you have not known--`and let us serve them, you shall not listen to the words of that prophet or that dreamer of dreams, for the Lord your God is testing you to know whether you love the Lord your God with all your heart."* (Deut. 13:1-3).

Being easily influenced is one of the causes that weaken the faith. Another reasons is:

6. Fear

Fear weakens faith and weak faith leads to fear. St. Peter, the great Apostle, denied Jesus out of fear. He insulted, cursed and swore that he didn't know the Man (Matt 26:74) and thus his faith weakened. Jesus told him before this occurred, *"...I have prayed for you, that your faith should not fail."* (Luke 22:32).

Many lose their faith due to fear. That is why the book of Revelation lists cowards as the first to perish, *"But the cowardly, unbelieving, abominable... shall have their part in the lake which burns with fire and brimstone."* (Rev. 21:8). The placement of the cowardly before the non-believers could mean that the cowardly, due to their fear, became non-believers.

Pontius Pilate, deep within himself, believed that Jesus was innocent of the charges made against Him by the Jews. He was confident that the Jews handed Him over due to envy. He tried to set Him free and said that he found no fault in Him. Despite this he finally submitted to his weakness and presented Jesus to be crucified because he was afraid what the people would say about him to Caesar (John 19:5-16).

As for the spiritual person, he doesn't lose his faith at all because he doesn't fear...

What also weakens faith is:

7. Lust

Many lost their faith due to lust. As an example of those is Demas, who was Paul's helper in service. Saint Paul wrote about him, *"Demas has forsaken me, having loved this present world..."* (2 Tim. 4:10). Love of the world weakens faith because it is hatred against God (James 4:4).

Also from the examples of those who lost their faith due to lust, was the rich young man. He left Christ, *"...sorrowful, for he had great possessions."* (Matt. 19:22). Thus, lust for money may weaken the faith.

How many left Jesus for the sake of a woman or a position... Solomon, the wisest on earth, lost his faith due to his lust for women. He, *"Loved many foreign women ... "* (1 Kin 11:1). *"...when Solomon was old, that his wives turned his heart after other gods; and his heart was not loyal to the Lord his God, as was the heart of his father David. For Solomon went after Ashtoreth the goddess of the Sidonians, and after Milcom the abomination of the Ammonites. Solomon did evil in the sight of the Lord."* (1 Kin 11:4-6).

This great wise man fell, however we believe that he repented in his last days. The book of Ecclesiasts is evidence to his repentance.

Ananias and Sapphira lost their faith for lust of money, so they perished.

They both lied to God (Acts 5:4) and also, *"...tested the Spirit of the Lord..."* (Acts 5:9). They both died and perished.

Balaam lost his faith due to his lust for money. He was a prophet and spoke beautiful prophecies about Jesus. Finally, he fell in darkness due to the, *"...wages of unrighteousness..."* (2 Pet. 2:15). He thus caused people to fall and taught Balak the way of sin (Rev. 2:14). He and others perished.

The lust for greatness and power lead to the loss of the faith of many. Maybe one of those was Diotrephes who, *"...who loves to have the preeminence among them..."*. Thus, he opposed Saint John and drove many brothers out of church (3 John 1:10)

The lust for Godliness lead the great Cherub to lose his faith and became a devil. Prior to this he was an angel of light with greatness and beauty.

Indeed lusts weaken and stop faith.

Other causes that weaken faith are distresses and the pressures of outer circumstances.

8. External Circumstances

As an example of such is Gideon. When his faith weakened concerning the care of God, the angel told him, *"The Lord is with you, you mighty man of valor!"* Gideon said to Him, *"O my lord, if the Lord is with us, why then has all this happened to us? And where are all His miracles which our fathers told us about, saying, 'Did not the Lord bring us up from Egypt?' But now the Lord has forsaken us and delivered us into the hands of the Midianites"?* (Judges 6:12-13).

If distresses prolong or becomes stronger, a person's faith could weaken.

The faith of the Disciples weakened and they doubted when the waves of the sea broke over the boat. They told the Lord, *"Do You not care that we are perishing?"* (Mark 4:38-40).

When the time that the Israelites were in bondage to Pharaoh was prolonged, they became discouraged and their faith that they would be freed weakened (Ex. 4:1).

There is another dangerous cause that weakens faith:

9. The Devil's Deceptions.

Among these deceptions are false visions. Satan often deceives us when he, *"...transforms himself into an angel of light."* (2 Cor. 11:14). He can even perform false miracles as it was said about the Antichrist at the end of time, *"...according to the working of Satan, with all power, signs and lying wonders, and with all unrighteous deception among those who perish."* (2 Thes. 2:9,10). The prophet said that this will cause the great rebellion before the coming of Christ (2 Thes. 2:3). Namely the loss of faith due to these Satanic deceptions.

Satan may deceive people with dreams, false prophecies, ideas, confusion and new teachings, so as to destroy their. He may even send them, *"...false prophets will rise and show great signs and wonders..."* (Matt. 24:24). He will try and convince you of a false Christ. The Lord warned, *"If anyone says to you, 'Look, here is the Christ!' or 'There!' do not believe it."* (Matt. 24:23).

All this needs discernment, as the Apostle wrote, *"Do not believe every spirit, but test the spirits, whether they are of God; because many false prophets have gone out into the world."* (1 John 4:1).

One of the main causes that weaken faith is:

10. Doubt

Doubt weakens faith and a weak faith produces doubt... This is exactly what we said about fear. Each of them causes the other or results from the other.

a) Doubt was one of the weapons the devil used against Adam and Eve in order to for them to lose their faith. He told them, *"Has God indeed said ... you will surely not die?* (Gen. 3:1-4).

If you are faced with doubts concerning the existence of God or other principle beliefs then do not fear. These are from the devil's wars and not because you have denied your faith and especially, if your heart was refusing it. In such circumstances, you have to pray for God to lift these wars from you and that you may change your way of thinking by occupying yourself with another subject. If doubts are from you and you are convinced of them so you have to treat them with a pure spiritual understanding by asking those who are righteous and trained in theology and by reading useful books on the subject.

There are other wars against doubt lighter than this, we mention the following:

b) Doubt in God's help or thinking that God has abandoned you.

The Lord rebukes this kind of doubt by saying, *"O you of little faith, why did you doubt?"* (Matt. 14:31). Here He shows the relationship between doubt and little faith because the person with a strong faith would never doubt in God's love and care.

The many continuing distresses may sometimes press on the heart and one would say, *"Why do You stand afar off, O Lord? Why do You hide in times of trouble?"* (Ps 10:1).

This is blame and not weakness in the faith. It seems to the Psalmist that the Lord is standing afar but the Lord keeps guard with all love and care for the security of His children. In this regard the Lord is like the eagle that teaches its youngsters to fly and like the father who teaches his son to swim. They leave them for a while to train and gain experience, yet they are watching with great care. If they see danger surrounding their children, they will hurry to rescue them.

There is also the example of the mother who teaches her son to walk. She leaves him to fall down and stand up again to strengthen his bones and muscles and to learn. However, if she hurried to carry him in her arms after each fall, he will not learn, his bones will not be strong enough and she will cripple him.

Trials is a school, in it we learn prayer and how to cling to God. In this school we are trained to abide in faith. Through it we are discover the strength of God and His marvelous works. Without a doubt God works, even if we do not see nor feel His miraculous touch.

The person may doubt if he only focuses on his troubles and not on God. That is what happened to St. Peter when he was walking on the water with Jesus. He looked to the water beneath his feet and did not see Jesus who held his hand. As the faith of St. Peter decreased so he started to sink and then the Lord rescued him.

The children of God may be 'lambs among wolves' but they do not doubt or fear. As long as the Good Shepherd is among the lambs no wolves or even lions will endanger them.

Our father Abram did not doubt in God's love and care, even when he was asked to sacrifice his son Isaac. Abram knew that God was more tender-hearted than himself toward Isaac and that God could manage Isaac's future better than he could. Abram knew that if God decided something then he has to agree with it because God has more wisdom and love that him.

He who does not doubt lives always in tranquility and peace.

He always lives in security and the outer circumstances will not make him anxious. He is not one to impose on God certain solutions, which if not carried out will make him angry. He agrees on any solution coming from God according to His Godly wisdom.

How many troubles do doubt cause in the heart and mind... like doubt, fear, disturbance and smallness of heart. Doubt in itself is tiresome and a burning fire.

Doubt is overcome by confidence and love. He who loves a person doesn't doubt in him. That is why we believe in God and do not doubt Him because we love Him and have confidence in Him. Our faith in Him doesn't allow us to doubt in His Godly and Fatherly deeds with us. Holy is He in all what He does.

Faith kills fear and doubt. Fear and doubt on the other side kill faith.

Hold on to your faith because it is a strong and victorious virtue. You will then live in joy, peace, tranquility, without fear, and without any doubt all the days of your life.

CHAPTER 10

THE TEST OF FAITH

Do You have Faith?

There are many measures to test your faith. They could be all deduced from the preceding chapters. In this chapter however, we will look deeper into the life of faith that was mentioned by the great Apostle St. Paul. He does not merely speak about faith, ie. to confine in the name of the Lord, but he specifically mentions the following:

1. Faith Expressing Itself Through Love (Gal. 5:6):

Test your faith through your love as described by the Apostle, *"Love suffers long and is kind; love does not envy; love does not parade itself, is not puffed up; does not behave rudely, does not seek its own, is not provoked, thinks no evil; does not rejoice in iniquity, but rejoices in the truth; bears all things, believes all things, hopes all things, endures all things."* (1 Cor. 13:4-7).

Do you have all these qualities that define faith? The Apostle said, *"...and though I have all faith, so that I could remove mountains, but have not love, I am nothing."* (1 Cor. 13:2). With this love, you can examine your faith. Yet in general, you can examine your faith through your deeds.

2. To Examine Faith Through Deeds

The Apostle says, *"...I will show you my faith by my works."* (James 2:18). Through deeds you can examine your faith if it is alive or dead because, *"...faith without works is dead."* (James 2:20) and a dead faith cannot save anyone (James 2:14).

St. Paul the Apostle, spoke a great deal about the importance of faith. He says, *"They profess to know God, but in works they deny Him."* (Titus 1:16). In his first letter to St. Timothy he stresses upon this point and says, *"But if anyone does not provide for his own, and especially for those of his household, he has denied the faith and is worse than an unbeliever."* (1 Tim. 5:8). The young widows forsook their dedication to Christ because, *"...they have cast off their first faith."* (1 Tim. 5:12). Those who love money, *"...have strayed from the faith..."* (1 Tim. 6:10) and those who are interested in impure and false chatter, *"...strayed concerning the faith."* (1 Tim. 6:21).

Therefore, the person's behaviour may be a test of his faith. St. John the Apostle said, *"He who says I know Him, and does not keep His commandments, is a liar, and the truth is not in him. "* (1 John 2:4), *"He who says he abides in Him ought himself also to walk just as He walked."* (1 John 2:6).

This brings us to the next point:

3. Examine Faith Through Purity of Heart

He who believes that God is in front of him, that God is holy and hates sin, that He is just and rewards everyone according to his deeds, fears to err in front of God, is ashamed to do any wrong and is ashamed to hurt the heart of God; If he does believe in God's love!.

Here the Apostle says, *"Whoever sins has neither seen Him nor known Him. ..."* (1 John 3:6). For sure, he who sins doesn't have in mind that God sees, hears and records everything while he sins and for sure he who does wrong doesn't completely believe that there is a God who, *"...gives freedom to the prisoners...."* (Ps 146:7). Hence, if one says to the one who is sinning, 'God exists', he fears and trembles.

For sure, the arrogant or proud person does not feel at all that he is standing in front of God. When Herod spoke to the people they praised him saying, *"This is the voice of a God, and not of man".* Herod was glad to hear this praise. He didn't have faith that God was in front of him and for this reason, *"...an angel of the Lord struck him ... And he was eaten by worms and died."* (Acts 12:21-23).

The true believer is one who practices religious devotion without envying the worldly things. The believers are content with whatever circumstances they are in (Phil. 4:1 1).

Another point in the life of faith is:

4. Faith Is Tested Through The Power It Grants That All Things Are Possible

Do you have the power of faith that you feel that anything is possible? As the Lord said, *"All things are possible to him who believes."* (Mark 9:23). Do you feel that something is hard or impossible? Or that your faith doesn't believe in God being able to do it? Do you doubt the matters that need miracles? Can you say what St. Paul the Apostle said, *"I can do all things through Christ who strengthens me."* (Phil. 4:13). Are you moved by obstacles and difficulties and think that their solution is impossible? Does despair fight you?

Despair is against faith and hope.

No doubt those who commit suicide have lost their faith and their hope. They felt that there was no solution. They also lost faith in life after death in eternity and their destiny in it.

Also those, who feel defeated by their present situation, to external pressures or to sin, didn't have any faith that there is power that can support and deliver them.

Faith is a power for those who can use it in confidence and without any doubt.

I fear that faith in the hand of some is used like the staff of Elisha in Gehazi's hand (2 Kin 4:31). I also fear the same thing concerning people who have a cross on their hands: they care to carry it and to perform its sign without having faith. They carry the cross but do not have the power that is concealed in it and in its work that can be shown through faith.

Do you think that Moses's rod split the Red sea? Or was it the faith of Moses carrying and using it in the name of the Lord? Do you have the power of faith that Moses had when he stretched his hand over the Red Sea?

You often pray but does your prayer have the faith that gives it strength? How wonderful is the Bible's saying about Elijah, *"...he prayed earnestly..."* (James 5:17). This prayer was not an ordinary prayer like that of the rest of the people because it could stop the heavens from giving rain and brought fire down from heaven.

Test your faith through the power you have as a result of your relationship with God.

5. Test Of Faith During Trials.

Trials face every person. There is a big difference between the way a believer and a non-believer deals with a trial. If the trial disturbs your peace then know that your faith is weak.

The believer accepts trials believing that they are for the good and that God will solve them. He is not disturbed or troubled and his heart is not burdened with sadness and pain.

He faces it with three verses; *"All things work together for good to those who love God..."* (Rom 8:28), *"Count it all joy when you fall into various trials... "* (James 2:1) and *"All things are possible to him who believes."* (Mark 9:23). With this faith, his heart rejoices in the trial and people are comforted through his happiness.

The believer places God between him and the trial; the trial disappears and God appears. He remembers God's hand with the saints in all their trials where, *"...the Angel of His Presence saved them... "* (Is 63:9). He remembers what happened to Moses, Joseph, David, Job, Daniel and the three saintly youth of Babylon. All these increase his faith, his confidence in God's intervention and in God's word. Thus he is not shaken in trials, he doesn't doubt, doesn't feel sad and doesn't feel anxious. Instead he says with the Psalmist, *"Our soul has escaped as a bird from the snare of the fowlers; The snare is broken, and we have escaped. Our help is in the name of the Lord, Who made heaven and earth."* (Ps 124).

He tells the Lord: 'As long as You allow this trial then I am content with it. I do not only accept it or approve of it but I am happy that the Lord gave me the blessing of this trial'. It is lovely what was said about the Apostles after being whipped, *"So they departed from the presence of the council, rejoicing that they were counted worthy to suffer shame for His name."* (Acts 5:41).

The believer sees the door of God open even though all the other doors seem to be closed.

He believes in God who has the keys of Heaven and earth, *"He who opens and no one shuts..."* (Rev. 3:7). The believer chants with St.

John saying, *"After these things I looked, and behold, a door standing open in heaven."* (Rev. 4:1). To test the faith is to see all doors open in front of you and every time you see a closed door in front of you, you are sure that this is not the door God wants me to go through. God has many other doors open. There are doors that are now closed but God will open them later on. With this faith you will be calm.

6. To Test Your Faith According To The Commandments:

a) A means of testing your faith is in your tithes and giving in general and especially when you yourself are in need or if you are asked to give from your belongings. The weak in faith would argue saying, 'If my whole salary doesn't suffice for my needs, then how can I make ends meet if it is reduced by a tenth?' The believer on the other hand has faith that if they give the tithe, the remainder will be blessed so that they will be able to support their needs and will even have excess.

The tithe is a spiritual test the Lord gave in the book of Malachi: *"Bring all the tithes into the storehouse, That there may be food in My house, And try Me now in this, Says the Lord of hosts, If I will not open for you the windows of heaven And pour out for you such blessing That there will not be room enough to receive it."* (Mal. 3:10). If the person - in spite of this Godly promise - doesn't pay, no doubt his faith is weak.

If a person has doubts about giving their tithes then how would they react to other commandments like, '...give to the one who asks you...' (Matt. 5:42) and *"...go, sell what you have and give to the poor..."* (Matt. 19:21) and *"...sell what you have and give alms..."* (Luke 12:33)?

In this way, your faith is tested: Is God capable of supporting you after you pay your share to the poor? Is He capable to support you without storing up treasures on earth (Matt. 6:19)?

b) Another Commandment that test your faith is to keep the Lord's day.

Do you rejoice in the Lord's day so that you can spend it with Him? Or do you prefer other occupations? Are material matters more important to you? It's a test of your faith.

c) Also an important tests is to what extent do you love prayer:

Do you forget it and have times when you don't pray? Does it happen that when you stand up for prayer you can't wait to finish because you want to occupy yourself with more interesting things? Does it happen that while you are praying your thoughts wander and you forget that you are standing in front of God talking to Him? If you are like that then your faith is not at all strong in God, in His companionship and in the pleasure of speaking with Him.

Likewise we could examine other prayer and spiritual practices to test our faith.

7. Test Your Faith By How Concerned You Are About Your Eternity.

Do you concentrate your mind and heart upon this world and how successful you are and how you enjoy yourself in it?

Are you interested in your eternity and your destiny in the other world and how you prepare yourself for it, as the Lord said, *"Let your waist be girded and your lamps burning; and you yourselves be like men who wait for their master, when he will return from the wedding, that when he comes and knocks they may open to him immediately. Blessed are those servants whom the master, when he comes, will find watching..."* (Luke 12:35-37).

The spiritual alertness is a deep test of faith.

Where is the faith of those who neglected their eternity? Where is their faith in the afterlife and their preparation for it with repentance and good deeds, with love and companionship with God and with oil in their lamps?

8. Test Your Faith By The Orthodoxy Of Your Belief

Is it a sound faith without controversy, false beliefs and foreign understandings? Is it the faith that was once entrusted to the saints (Jude 3) and to reliable men who were also qualified to teach others (2 Tim.2:12). Is it in accordance with the teachings of the Bible, or do you follow people who spread their own teachings? By answering these questions you can test your faith. This is important because belief has a practical effect on the spiritual life.

9. Test Your Faith Whether it Has Sound Qualities

Is your faith a practical one? Is it firm so that no outer circumstances can shake it? Does it weaken or does it have doubt? Is it filled with peace and does not fear? Do you know the life of submission and the obedience of faith? Is your faith a living and prosperous one? Does it grow and increase?

I don't want to mention the rest of the qualities of faith so that you can test them yourself.

But if you want more measures, you can read this book again from the beginning.

CPSIA information can be obtained
at www.ICGtesting.com
Printed in the USA
BVHW060206180220
572581BV00011B/1414